BUILDING
BETTER IDEAS

BUILDING
BETTER
IDEAS

How Constructive Debate Inspires Courage,
Collaboration, and Breakthrough Solutions

B. Kim Barnes

BK

Berrett–Koehler Publishers, Inc.

Berrett-Koehler Publishers, Inc.
1333 Broadway, Suite 1000
Oakland, CA 94612-1921
Tel: (510) 817-2277
Fax: (510) 817-2278
www.bkconnection.com

ORDERING INFORMATION
Quantity sales. Special discounts are available on quantity purchases by corporations, associations, and others. For details, contact the "Special Sales Department" at the Berrett-Koehler address above.
Individual sales. Berrett-Koehler publications are available through most bookstores. They can also be ordered directly from Berrett-Koehler:
Tel: (800) 929-2929; Fax: (802) 864-7626; www.bkconnection.com.
Orders for college textbook / course adoption use.
Please contact Berrett-Koehler: Tel: (800) 929-2929; Fax: (802) 864-7626.

Distributed to the U.S. trade and internationally by Penguin Random House Publisher Services.

Berrett-Koehler and the BK logo are registered trademarks of Berrett-Koehler Publishers, Inc.

Printed in the United States of America.

Berrett-Koehler books are printed on long-lasting acid-free paper. When it is available, we choose paper that has been manufactured by environmentally responsible processes. These may include using trees grown in sustainable forests, incorporating recycled paper, minimizing chlorine in bleaching, or recycling the energy produced at the paper mill.

Library of Congress Cataloging-in-Publication Data

Names: Barnes, B. Kim, author.
Title: Building better ideas : how constructive debate inspires courage, collaboration, and breakthrough solutions / B. Kim Barnes.
Description: 1st Edition. | Oakland, CA : Berrett-Koehler Publishers, [2019] | Includes bibliographical references and index.
Identifiers: LCCN 2019013267 | ISBN 9781523085583 (paperback)
Subjects: LCSH: Teams in the workplace. | Communication in personnel management. | Debates and debating. | Leadership.
Classification: LCC HD66 .B367 2019 | DDC 658.4/022—dc23
LC record available at https://lccn.loc.gov/2019013267

First Edition

25 24 23 22 21 20 19   10 9 8 7 6 5 4 3 2 1

Book producer: Westchester Publishing Services
Text designer: Courtney Baker
Cover designer: Paula Goldstein

This book is dedicated to the memory of Margaret Fuller, an American journalist, author, and promoter of intelligent "Conversations" among men and women in the early nineteenth century. A friend of Ralph Waldo Emerson, Henry David Thoreau, Horace Mann, and other luminaries of her time, she sought recognition for women as intellectual equals and encouraged her friends and those she mentored, male and female, to speak up and speak out on important questions of her era.

I also dedicate this book to my supportive team and associates at Barnes & Conti, especially Rebecca Hendricks, who worked closely with me to develop the concepts discussed in this book. Rebecca offers me the essential combination of support and challenge whenever we collaborate. I am grateful for all our constructive debates.

B. Kim Barnes

Contents

BUILDING
BETTER IDEAS

Introduction

Why Do We Always Have to Have
"The Meeting *After* the Meeting?"

It's three o'clock. Your product development team meeting has just ended. And here you are in the break room with most of the other team members.

"*Can you believe what Jason just proposed?*"
"*I can. It's the same thing he's proposed for the last four meetings.*"
"*Only the names were changed to protect the guilty!*"
"*Does he even know what century we're in? That's three product cycles ago, for two of our competitors.*"
"*I could have told him that idea will never fly in today's market.*"
"*I have a much better idea, but he'd never go for it.*"
"*So, why didn't anybody say anything?*"
"*He's the boss.*"
Meanwhile, near the manager's office . . .

"Nobody had any ideas today, as usual. I think people are just checked out."
"Maybe we need some different people—more creative ones?"
"I doubt that we could attract any real *innovators. The culture seems to reward people who don't rock the boat."*

If any of this sounds familiar, you're not alone. Ideas are the life-blood of organizations in the current climate; but having a constant flow of new and interesting ideas to explore, develop, test, and bring to market is not a given. Three major factors contribute to the dearth of great ideas:

- First, few ideas are great to begin with. They have to be questioned, critiqued, improved, and developed, and then they must compete with other ideas for support, commitment, and resources.
- Second, few people have been well trained in the skills that enable them to work with their own and others' ideas in a tough, honest, competitive, and yet collaborative way.
- And third, organizational politics, tribal loyalties, and human emotions such as fear of loss are a powerful, yet sometimes invisible, factor in communication and decision-making within organizations.

What Do We Mean When We Use the Word "Idea"?

An idea, at least in the sense we use the word in organizations, is a thought or opinion that is formulated and can be expressed. Ideas are the way we frame our thinking about a specific topic. Some ideas are fixed—we form them early and seldom change them. They become part of our worldview and are the basis for testing the truth of other information or opinions. Other ideas are more tentative, less solid, and open to new experiences, experiments, or the influence of other people.

In a time when innovation—that is, creating value from an idea that's new to you—is key to the success of many organizations, high-quality ideas are an extremely valuable currency. In fact, they are the raw material for innovation. Paul Romer, a co-winner of the 2018 Nobel Prize in Economic Sciences, has shown that new ideas are the fuel for long-term economic growth and that organizations need to invest in research and development. They also need to support improved patent laws to encourage innovation.[1] Those investments can best pay off when potential innovators thrive in welcoming environments. Organizations will risk obsolescence or failure if they can't respond with new and powerful ideas to customer needs, changing technology, social and cultural movements, competitive pressure, political or environmental crises, and unexpected opportunities.

So, Whose Job Is It to Generate Ideas?

While generating ideas is seldom part of a formal job description, it's hard to think of a job where that skill wouldn't be relevant. Anyone who has worked in an organization will be aware that a large proportion of problems that frontline employees face will never reach the senior executive level. It's common wisdom that those who are closest to the problem or opportunity are in the best position to deal with it. If the only person with the responsibility and permission to generate ideas is a formal leader or a designated professional, there are probably too many people in the "room." Any organization can benefit from a workforce that is both expected to be and skillful in being creative and forthcoming with suggestions and proposals.

A few years ago, a large client organization approached me with a need that they described in the following way: "We need to get rid of the 'meeting after the meeting' where people discuss what they *really* thought and felt during the actual meeting, but didn't say. We want to help our people stop bad ideas from getting a pass, and then encourage them to put new ideas forward, even if they might be partial and 'unbaked'—or at least very different from our current common wisdom. Can you develop a training program that would help with this?"

On hearing the presenting issues, I first explored with them the possibility that they were looking for skills in interpersonal or intergroup communication or perhaps in conflict resolution. While my own company had existing programs in those arenas, it soon became clear to all of us that the issue was not really conflict, but rather the *fear* of conflict or of loss—loss of security, status, or relationship, for example. This fear suppressed people's willingness to suggest unusual or innovative ideas or to risk criticizing ideas promoted by leaders. I suggested that there may not have been any actual conflict to manage or resolve. In fact, the client group described the organizational culture as "conflict-averse." Next, I inquired whether a better set of influencing skills (also a specialty of my company) might be useful. In fact, they thought the primary approach to getting their people to agree was power, whether used overtly, or below the radar, or even unconsciously. While influence skills might have been useful, once some interesting ideas had been put out there to compete for support, the real problems were that the ideas laid on the table—often by senior managers or those who wanted to curry favor with them—tended to be obvious, weak, or traditional, and that little effort was made to criticize or improve them. Once a leader mentioned or approved of an idea, other ideas rarely emerged from the group.

Clearly, leaders in that organization needed to do a much better job of inviting and welcoming alternatives, while at the same time the company culture needed to become more supportive of engagement and healthy competition of ideas. Perhaps because of the existing climate, team members appeared to have a skills deficit. When I identified an apparent unwillingness, inhibition, or inability on the part of many team members to risk speaking up to make bad ideas better, or to develop small ideas into robust ones (without provoking interpersonal conflict), the client agreed that this situation was worth targeting for improvement. My team would work on skill development, but we would also do our best to help them move their culture toward one that welcomed constructive discussion, disagreement, and debate, all the while supporting their strategic initiatives related to change and innovation.

Why Don't People Speak Up?

Organizational or team cultures that discourage disagreement and debate risk missing ideas that could transform their business results, create greater efficiency, or help them to become a great place to work, attracting the best talent. Those ideas, or at least the seeds of them, walk out the actual or virtual door of their company every day between the ears of team members. Worse, ignoring, not requesting, or not providing honest feedback can lead to disastrous results, financial or otherwise. Serious errors of judgment can, and do, occur when people assume that those who are senior to them in rank or experience can never be questioned. When people who wish to express unusual or unpopular ideas and opinions are silenced, directly or indirectly, disasters can and do happen.

In a classic example of this, the Rogers Commission report[2] on the causes of the spaceship *Challenger*'s fatal accident in 1986, stated:

> . . . failures in communication . . . resulted in a decision to launch 51-L [Challenger] based on incomplete and sometimes misleading information, a conflict between engineering data and management judgments, and a NASA management structure that permitted internal flight safety problems to bypass key Shuttle managers.

Morton Thiokol, an engineering company involved in building the *Challenger*, was at that time hoping to win more contracts with NASA. The company's senior managers did not listen to the engineers on the project when they stated their safety concerns about the shuttle's O-rings. The senior managers—who actually knew about the issues and could have stopped the launch—made the fatal decision to agree to go ahead with it. The lack of major checks and balances, the hope for additional business, and the hierarchical nature of the decision-making at both Morton Thiokol and NASA at the time meant that those in the best position to know about the risks were not listened to. As a result, seven crew members died.

During the U.S. Senate hearing that concluded with the Rogers Report, two of the engineers responded as follows:

"I was not even asked to participate. I did not agree. . . . I was never asked or polled, it was clearly a management position. There was no point in me doing anything further. I really did all I could to stop the launch."

"I remember distinctly at the time [wondering] whether I would have the courage if asked, what I would do . . . whether I would be alone. . . . I didn't think I'd be alone, but I was wondering if I would have the courage, I remember that distinctly, to stand up and say 'No.'"

When neither alternative solutions nor critical feedback are invited or welcomed in an organization, it's almost inevitable that certain consequences will result: Resources will be wasted on mediocre ideas that fail or don't perform as hoped, and talented people with better ideas will eventually take those ideas elsewhere.

Many leaders do things, intentionally or not, that discourage their own people from weighing in openly on ideas or decisions. The leaders may begin discussions by announcing their own proposals, seeking agreement rather than a critique or a number of alternatives. They may become defensive when their assumptions are challenged or their rationale is questioned. Or they may run with the first halfway-decent idea expressed by a team member, instead of probing for other ideas so that the group would have a variety to choose from. They may, without even being aware of their actions or motives, favor people who agree with them and punish those with different opinions. This sends a message to others in the group or team about what is safe and "politically correct."

At the same time, many team members may lack experience, skill, or the confidence in their ability to speak up, to disagree, and to initiate or participate in a robust discussion—what we will come to call a "constructive debate": one that can lead to better, stronger, and more successful ideas.

Are teams in your organization making great decisions? Do they consider alternative, even competing, points of view before they decide to act? Are the right people invited in to the process, and then really listened to? Do team members build on one another's ideas to improve them? Do teams avoid playing politics and instead keep a rigorous focus on developing promising concepts and solutions? Do members avoid defensiveness and ask for feedback? Can creative, unusual, and even risky ideas get a hearing? Can people disagree and remain good colleagues? Or, is your organization one where "the meeting after the meeting" is the norm—a follow-up event in which people express their *real* opinions after they have allowed a suboptimal or mediocre idea to move forward? Is yours an organization whose people typically hesitate to disagree openly with conventional wisdom, an organization where fear of failure or even minor conflict means that potentially great ideas may never get expressed?

As a formal or informal leader, you are in a position to help change the culture—the norms and practices that govern the way the people you lead behave. Whether as a trusted advisor, business partner, organizational consultant, coach, change leader, or facilitator, you can support and promote a culture where "constructive debate" becomes the norm.

So, How Does This Apply to Me?

A constructive debate is one in which a diverse group of individuals can express their ideas, engage others in building on and improving them, explore ideas deeply, and challenge one another's positions in a fair and productive way.

In this book, you'll learn a set of behaviors you can model and encourage, as well as a process you can facilitate, lead, or support your client in leading. The process enables a group or team to:

- consider a variety of ideas before making a decision
- invite the expression of diverse points of view
- avoid "groupthink" and "playing it safe"
- discourage defensiveness and promote feedback on ideas
- encourage both creative and critical thinking
- support collaborative exploration of problems and opportunities

- confront difficult issues while averting interpersonal conflict
- identify, explore, and develop promising ideas

You'll learn how an organization can experience a culture change through applying this process, and you'll have an opportunity to practice some skills and outline a design for a constructive debate that needs to occur in your organization.

In the following chapters, we'll explore the concept and practice of "constructive debate," and present ways that you can implement, facilitate, and support it. We'll examine how organizational culture and leadership behavior can affect individuals' willingness to take the risk of contributing unusual or creative ideas or to critique and improve suboptimal ideas before they are implemented. In today's difficult social and political climate, when opinions can often be tribal and differences can lead to unconstructive conflict, it's important to find ways to build robust ideas through a thoughtful, fair, and inclusive process. You can help that to happen.

PART ONE

WHERE ARE THE GOOD IDEAS?

The Need for Constructive Debate

1 ■ What Is Constructive Debate?

Building better ideas should be a constructive activity—both metaphorically and in the real world. The word "constructive" connotes positive and productive action. The word "debate" sometimes connotes dissonance or disagreement, but also suggests a rational process aimed at achieving a clear understanding or decision. The two words together suggest a course of action designed to create something strong through deep and energetic deliberation.

Debate versus Discussion

Why do we call this process and skill-set "debate" rather than "discussion" or "dialogue"? A discussion is a conversation for the purpose of making a decision or exchanging views. A dialogue is a discussion for the purpose of coming to an understanding of an issue rather than making a decision. The word "debate" indicates that there are disagreements or different opinions on a topic.

Whether informal or formal (following a set of specific rules), a debate is a discussion in which contending views are expressed and responded to.

Debate as a form of communication, rather than as a formal activity with judges making the decision as to the winners and losers, is often focused not so much on the construction of a good argument as on the demolition of another's position. This often results in a heated exchange that may or may not solve a problem or advance the interests of the organization. Typically, informal debate, when it is focused on making the other person wrong, stimulates defensive rather than productive behavior. It can discourage those with different—perhaps innovative—views and less taste for battle.

Constructive Debate

By contrast, constructive debate involves the open exchange and exploration of ideas in a way that promotes innovation, high-quality decisions, broad participation, and relationships that are both positive and productive. In any organization, people often come to the table with opinions that are formed—sometimes even fixed. We rarely begin with completely open minds, which would allow us to discuss a topic in a completely impartial way. Ideally, however, we can establish a set of principles and a process that allow us to set aside our own preferences for long enough to give contending ideas a real hearing.

Constructive debate is a form of communication that is:

- rational rather than emotional
- based on facts and logic rather than opinion and belief
- interactive rather than sequential
- focused on bringing promising ideas to the table, then testing, developing, and improving them

Criteria for a Constructive Debate

A constructive debate looks, sounds, and feels very different from an argument that is focused on blame and "one-upmanship." It is more collaborative than a formal debate where the goal is to score points against the other side. During a constructive debate:

- It is relatively easy for each participant to express an opinion.
- A broad range of opinions and ideas is expressed and considered.
- Discussion/debate is focused on the ideas, not on motivation, personality, or history.
- Participants ask for and receive feedback nondefensively.
- Participants build on one another's ideas.
- Participants challenge their own as well as others' thinking.
- Ideas are explored fully enough to warrant moving toward narrowing and decision-making.

Issues that Require Constructive Debate

Many day-to-day issues can be resolved by precedent (as in "We don't need to reinvent the wheel") or handled in an ad-hoc way ("I'll try it this way today"). When dealing with issues that are key to team or organizational success, especially those involving innovation or change, a constructive debate can greatly increase the likelihood of a positive outcome.

Innovation and change require examination of unusual and sometimes unpopular ideas, so debate that is open and constructive offers an opportunity to build better ideas and decisions through opening our minds to more possibilities. In a formal debate, a third party—the debate judge—makes a decision about the "winner." In a constructive debate about actual issues or opportunities, the group itself may come to a decision based on criteria, or they may simply make recommendations based on the result of their interaction. Not all decisions require a constructive debate.

Here are some criteria for issues that can benefit from this practice:

- There is no "school solution" or single right answer.
- Critical thinking is possible; facts and logic apply—it is not just a matter of opinion.

- Your intention is to develop ideas that are relevant to important strategic goals.
- You are aware that political pressure or "groupthink" could lead to a less-than-optimal decision.

The promise of constructive debate, when practiced regularly and with a supportive culture and set of processes, is better ideas, improved decision-making, greater collaboration and engagement, more successful innovation, broader commitment to decisions, and fewer unintended negative consequences.

2 ■ How Do We Form Ideas and Arrive at a Position?

Before we explore the process and skills involved in constructive debate, let's spend some time thinking about how we develop and communicate our ideas. Although most of us are trained to value objectivity, much of our communication is actually based on our own subjective interpretation of events. We react to these interpretations, which we will call assumptions, by making value judgments; these judgments are often followed by an emotional response. All this gets communicated to others. Linguistics, the scientific study of language, has developed some useful concepts that can help us understand the structure of communication.

Worldview

Each of us has a unique way of looking at the world. This can be compared to a particular set of lenses or a map of the world to which we continuously refer. We develop our worldview through family, culture, language, education, profession, industry, and the many other influences to which we are exposed, especially in our formative years. A Swede sees snow differently from a Floridian. A geologist looks at rocks differently from a rock climber. A finance person looks at customers differently from the way a salesperson does.

Deep Structure: Generalizations, Deletions, and Distortions

As we observe the "objective" world, we view it through our own lenses or filters. Our everyday environment is like water to a fish—it's just there; we don't take note of it. Most of the time, we're not particularly conscious of what we consider normal activities, since we already have a place for them on our mental map; they fall into familiar categories. We have a tendency, as linguists have shown, to generalize from what we know to what we don't know—and either to distort or to delete (edit out) anything that doesn't make sense, given that view. All snow may look alike to Floridians; their experience does not provide a "map" for differentiation, so differences in the type of snow are ignored. Swedes or Aleuts, on the other hand, have the worldview, including the language, to distinguish among many different kinds of snow. Deleting or distorting that information would cause them real inconvenience. In a famous "selective attention" experiment at Harvard University a number of years ago,[3] researchers Christopher Chabris and Daniel Simon demonstrated that when subjects were asked to count basketball passes shown on a brief video, half of them didn't notice the person in the gorilla suit walking past the players. When asked afterward if they would have noticed such a thing, most of them were sure that they would, but then felt surprised to discover that they had ignored it—in fact, had deleted it.

Generalization, deletion, and distortion are examples of what linguists call the "deep structure" of communication. It consists of the basic mental maps or models each of us has of reality. We develop these models over the course of our lives; they are almost always below our awareness, but they influence all our thinking and communication. We do not act directly on the world, in other words;

we act on our *model* of the world. These models are both focusing and limiting. Generalization means that we assume that everything that is like our model in some characteristics is like it in all characteristics. Deletion means that we leave out of our perception things that don't fit the model. Distortion means that we actually see or hear something different from "reality" in order to make it fit our model. In fact, the nature of objective reality has come under question in recent years from both ends of the political spectrum. We pick and choose (or create) the "facts" that best fit our beliefs or needs.

Facts, Assumptions, and Values

To communicate effectively, it's important to be able to distinguish among facts, assumptions, and values. As we reflect on how we or others reach a conclusion, it's useful to note the differences among these three types of statements or self-talk:

- Facts are data that can be objectively observed; for example, *"The marketing manager has been meeting with the finance manager for over two hours."*
- Assumptions are the meanings we assign to the observed facts; for example, *"There must be a problem in funding our new project."*
- Values are positive or negative beliefs or judgments in response to our assumptions; for example, *"The marketing manager should have worked that issue out before announcing the new project."* Values are often expressed through opinions that are based on our assumptions or preferences, rather than on facts.

Managing Your Assumptions

We can never completely manage our assumptions; they are a part of us. It is said that "the eye cannot see itself"; so it is with assumptions. When we don't distinguish among facts, assumptions, and the value judgments we make based on those assumptions, we operate as if our assumptions were the truth—that is, objective reality. This limits our ability to communicate with others, both in expressing our own ideas and in receiving information and ideas from them. This also limits the quality and variety of our ideas. Critical thinking is enhanced when we recognize that we operate with a worldview that leads us to make certain assumptions. When communicating about something significant, we can make our assumptions explicit to ourselves and others; this allows us to test them. When we are developing important ideas, we're often communicating with people who hold at least somewhat different worldviews from our own. As a part of this process, it's important to find common ground as well as to explore differences; this can only be accomplished if we're willing to have an open discussion about the assumptions that each of us hold about the matter at hand.

How We Arrive at a Position

In most informal debates, participants enter with a position on the issue under consideration. They have arrived at their positions either through a process of reasoning or through adopting the position that best meets their underlying needs. It's useful to deconstruct how these positions develop. The organizational psychologist Chris Argyris[4] of Harvard University described the process of reasoning as occurring on a "ladder of inference":

- *Observable data:* At the bottom of the ladder of inference are all the data related to our topic of interest.
- *Selected data:* We filter the data through our culture, values, needs, experience, language, or belief system, and then we select specific data to notice.
- *Interpretation:* We assign meaning to our observations, placing them in a context that is familiar to us.
- *Assumptions:* We make certain assumptions based on our interpretation of the data.
- *Conclusions:* We draw conclusions from the assumptions. These conclusions may, over time, become fixed beliefs

that then act as additional filters. Finally, we take actions based on the conclusions.

According to Argyris's research, most of the time, we move up that ladder too quickly to take account of the steps along the way, thus causing us to confuse facts, values, and assumptions. We quickly integrate new information with our existing assumptions and may use the result to further justify our previous decisions or actions. The decisions we then make or the actions we then choose may bear only a slight relationship to all the relevant data available. Different people may select a different set of data, assign different meanings to it, and arrive at quite different conclusions.

In a constructive debate, we attempt to make this process visible both to ourselves and to others, thereby creating an opportunity to exchange information and ideas based on the same data, as well as to develop alternative ways of framing the information and to open up a variety of possible conclusions.

The same process occurs when a group or team is engaged in a debate or discussion. The team often allows the content of the discussion to stay at the top of the ladder, rather than "drilling down" to uncover the source of a suggestion or conclusion. The constructive debate skills we will be describing are based on the idea (really, an assumption!) that by making the thinking process more transparent and testable, the ideas that emerge will be more robust.

Avoiding Unconscious Bias and Other Thinking Errors

In recent years, we have become more aware of the role that unconscious bias plays in decision-making by both groups and individuals. We can think of these biases as errors in thinking. These errors usually involve confusion or lack of distinction among facts, assumptions, values, beliefs, or preferences. Certain thinking errors occur frequently in both business and personal decision-making. Unfortunately, they can be extremely costly to businesses and careers. Some aspects of organizational culture can even support these errors in thinking. Cultural values and norms can be very positive, but if leaders are not careful in interpreting them, they may work against strategic and critical thinking. For example:

- A bias toward alignment and teamwork can lead to "groupthink" and to avoidance of necessary and healthy conflict of ideas and principles.
- A focus on business results, especially short-term results, can lead to practices that optimize near-term gains but lead to unanticipated long-term problems or losses.
- An emphasis on strong leadership or a culture that is overly focused on specialist knowledge (while devaluing the broader knowledge of leaders who are generalists) can lead to a narrow focus on one person's ideas, goals, and points of view.

Individuals may make or accept these errors in their business thinking for reasons that include personal advantage or gain, a desire to be accepted or respected, a wish to avoid conflict, a preference for answers that align with one's own values or vested interests, or simply a preference for simple solutions that don't require much effort. Here are a few of the most common errors:

Confirmation bias: a tendency to seek information that supports our expectations and to believe the information that supports our biases.

- Example: *The fact that our customers didn't complain about the last batch proves that we have solved our quality issues.*

Popularity bias: a tendency to believe that something is true because so many (or so many of the "right" people) believe it to be so. This can be part of a need for belonging to a particular social group or "tribe."

- Example: *Everyone I know thinks we should not do this— who am I to disagree?*

Hasty generalizations: a tendency to base conclusions on a very small or unrepresentative sample.

- Example: *"We tried that once, and it didn't go over well—it just would never work here."*

Wishful thinking: a tendency to believe that something is true because we want it to be so or because it would serve our vested interests.

- Example: *"We have the best salesforce in the country, so it won't be a big problem if we are late to market."*

Rationalization: a tendency to start with the conclusion and seek evidence to support it (similar to confirmation bias and sometimes called the "sunk costs" fallacy).

- Example: *"We have already made a big commitment to this approach; it would be too expensive to start over again. Besides, we'd look wishy-washy."*

Adversarial bias/ad hominem arguments: a tendency to dismiss or devalue the ideas of those we don't like or respect or whom we see as adversaries, regardless of their ideas' actual merits. This error attacks the person instead of focusing on the idea.

- Example: *"Why would I believe anything Janet says? She always exaggerates."*

Circular reasoning (sometimes called begging the question): assuming the truth of something that has not been proved and then using that "truth" as an argument to support one's point.

- Example: *"We are taking this action because it's the right thing to do."*

The way to prevent these and other fallacies from becoming key elements in important business decisions is to structure meetings and decision processes so that both leaders and team members are encouraged to question assumptions, seek a variety of opinions, and support their proposals with clear logic and appropriate data. Most organizations have a version of the old Army saying: "We don't have time to do it right, but we have time to do it over." In these days of closer scrutiny of business decisions, we may not have the luxury of doing it over. Strategic decisions ought to be made in a thoughtful, unbiased, and ethical way.

To put convincing arguments forward, we need to examine our thinking objectively and critically, as uncomfortable as that may often be. Likewise, in building and maintaining an environment that supports and encourages thoughtful and constructive debate, leaders must encourage team members to dispute points based on both the quality of the data and the merit of the thinking behind the argument.

To hold a truly constructive debate, participants would do well to examine their own thinking objectively. Likewise, in creating and maintaining an environment that supports and encourages constructive debate, leaders ought to encourage their team members to dispute points based on the accuracy and relevance of the data as well as on the quality of the thinking behind the argument.

3 ■ Power, Fear, Apathy, and Groupthink

Why Do Bad Ideas Get a Pass?

Meanwhile, back in the breakroom . . .

"Why didn't anybody say anything? You know that idea will never work."

"For the same reason that you were quiet . . . what good would it do? Del would simply argue with you, you'd end up with a bad review, and nothing would change."

The Problem with Employee Engagement

In recent studies of employee engagement (or lack thereof), futility is often cited as the reason people don't speak up in meetings. Employees sense that nothing will change when they provide a critique or offer alternatives. The decision has been made, they believe, and the attempt to involve them is a sham—and can only lead to trouble for the person naive enough to accept the invitation. The result is apathy and lack of engagement.

To be fair, many managers and leaders genuinely want to hear a response from team members about their ideas and decisions. Unfortunately, too many of them are so convinced they are right that they avoid or reject any disconfirming feedback. They hope—even expect—that team members will agree and thus buy in, support, and execute on their idea. I have often heard managers say of their people, "I want them to think that it's *their* idea." (Of course, this seldom works—unless it is, in fact, their idea.) Managers may fear that letting people know that a decision has been made without their input will make that manager come across as authoritarian. They have not yet grasped that faking openness leads to cynicism.

The conditions for real employee engagement in creating ideas include: 1) that a decision has not yet been made and 2) that the senior person is actually open to being influenced about it. For example, say a manager informs employees about an upcoming move. The decision has been made and there is no opportunity to change it. If you're that manager, rather than asking what your employees think about it, why not ask how it will affect them and what support they will need from you and upper management? These are genuine questions that offer your employees a chance to shape how the move can successfully happen.

Example: *"The board has made a final decision on the move. It will occur over the next six months. I know this will be disruptive to many of you and I'd like to know what you expect the main issues to be in your department. Then I'd like you to tell me what you think we should do to get ready and how I can be most helpful to you and your teams."*

Power

In any group, even when no one with formal authority happens to be present, some people have or display more power than others. It may be based on seniority, expertise, gender, closeness to the leadership, self-confidence, likeability, charisma, or even height. Some of these factors may actually be relevant to the topic under consideration—and others, not so much. It's useful to recognize that, if you're a person who carries power in the group, you need to make sure it doesn't detract from the task of building, considering, and deciding on the best or most promising ideas.

New York University Stern Professors Elizabeth Morrison and Kelly See, along with coauthor Caitlin Pan of SIM University, found that a major contributing factor to employees' unwillingness to speak up is a sense of powerlessness. In their article "An Approach-Inhibition Model of Employee Silence: The Joint Effects of Personal Sense of Power and Target Openness,"[5] they recommend that supervisors find ways to reduce the power differential and to communicate their genuine openness to others' ideas.

Leaders and others with power, whether the formal or the informal kind, often transmit signals as to what they prefer, even when they think they are really being open-minded. Those signals can be verbal, such as offering immediate praise ("Great idea!"), or nonverbal, such as scowling or looking away when they dislike something that's said. Leaders are often surprisingly unaware of the impact of their power and how closely team members and others read signals about what they are expecting or hoping to hear. In particular, managers seldom notice how their approval of specific ideas early in an ideation process can affect and narrow the course of a discussion.

To minimize this, you as a leader can withhold your opinion until your team members have spoken, and also do what you can to manage your expressions and voice tone. For instance, in an in-person meeting you can sit in a less observable place and focus your attention and interest on what others are saying. Listening actively to many different ideas (not just the ones you prefer) sends a different kind of signal—that you are receptive to considering many options. Simply stating that you are "open to ideas" is insufficient; you have to demonstrate it.

Power can also be managed through the design of a meeting. For example, sometimes having people generate ideas within smaller subgroups and report them out for consideration can spread the risk and thereby reduce concerns about speaking out. This is especially useful in cultures or subcultures where authority is deeply respected, as well as in groups where many people are more introverted and feel uncomfortable speaking out alone.

The Fear Factor

One of the most potent agents in depressing engagement and limiting the scope of a discussion is the fear factor. Fear of loss of a job, status, relationship, opportunity, or even respect can cause us to play it safe. Especially in an organizational culture that is more hierarchical, speaking truth to power may not be the best route to individual career success. However, if it is taboo, the organization loses the chance to benefit from all the brainpower in the actual or virtual room. Punishing people for questioning "politically correct" or "expert" solutions will quickly extinguish that behavior.

Asking people to express dissenting views—even when they do it as a kind of warmup exercise—can reduce this kind of fear. If leaders or managers request opposing or alternative views in order to test and improve an idea, and then consistently respond in an appreciative, nondefensive way (they need not agree), people will be more willing to express doubts or to suggest other options. When disagreement is framed as a helpful aspect of exploring new ideas rather than as disrespectful, insubordinate, a form of interpersonal conflict, or simply an impediment to progress, the cultural norms can change to support a forum that is both collaborative and competitive. In this way, weaker ideas can be rejected in favor of a better option or can be tested, improved on, and made ready for a solid decision process.

Groupthink

Irving Janis,[6] a Yale research social psychologist, identified the phenomenon of "groupthink" through studies in the 1970s—so the business world has been familiar with the idea for some time. It doesn't seem to have disappeared. Groupthink is what happens when a group overvalues harmony and agreement and avoids conflict by quickly agreeing to a proposal or point of view to reduce the discomfort of having to work through a critical evaluation of dissenting positions. If being a "team player" is culturally defined as going along with the leader or the majority, groupthink will be the result. If, however, the definition of a team player is someone who both supports and challenges others' thinking, a different standard can become common.

Some ways of breaking through "groupthink" when it occurs, are the following:

- Generate additional ideas. You can even assign a specific number, as in *"Let's come up with ten different ideas in the next five minutes."*
- Assign subgroups to come up with either support for the idea or objections to it (regardless of their personal opinions).
- Ask *"What are we assuming in order to see this as the best solution?"* Then ask *"What might we consider if we didn't make that assumption?"*
- Make sure your group is as diverse as possible in order to invite various points of view and reduce the likelihood of groupthink. Diversity can mean differences in professional background, position or status, gender, membership in a team or business unit, geographic location, generation or age, thinking style, or many other factors.

We human beings, like other social animals, prefer harmony within our group. Many laboratory studies have affirmed the strength of group pressure to conform. Our cultural mythology celebrates heroism, but is less enthusiastic about martyrdom. And not everyone with good ideas is willing to set off the "organizational immune reaction" (discussed in part 3).

The Value of Diversity

A diverse group or team will typically make better decisions, according to research cited in *Forbes Magazine* and in *Harvard Business Review.*[7]

According to the research, teams outperform individual decision makers 66% of the time, and decision-making improves as team diversity increases. Compared to individual decision makers, all-male teams make better business decisions 58% of the time, while gender diverse teams do so 73% of the time. Teams that also include a wide range of ages and different geographic locations make better business decisions 87% of the time.

Of course, there are many kinds of diversity. When making important decisions, you can be thoughtful in soliciting ideas from people with a variety of backgrounds, whose education, experiences, views, ways of thinking, or assumptions differ widely and therefore may have value related to a particular topic.

WHERE ARE THE IDEAS?

The Madrigal Company manufactures high-end yogurt. They were founded about 25 years ago, during a time when their competition was mostly from large food and beverage corporations. Madrigal's products stood out as healthier and more sophisticated. Their primary markets include specialty grocery stores, hotels, and restaurants. They also have a website where individual customers can order in bulk. They use organic ingredients and pride themselves on high-quality products and environmental responsibility in their processes. In recent years, though, they have seen their market share begin to diminish. Even though yogurt has become a staple of North American diets, which initially boosted sales, many new domestic and foreign competitors have entered the market at a similar level with excellent products. Madrigal needs to find ways to differentiate, rebuild its brand, and find additional markets. It really needs some big new ideas. Recent meetings to generate new product ideas have not produced anything out of the ordinary—in fact, several of them had to be killed after customer testing revealed a "blah!" reaction.

The company's business culture is relatively traditional. The original founder, Ellen Madrigal, is still the CEO, and she has a tradition of treating employees like "family"—as a result, many of them stay with Madrigal for a long time. Recently, Ellen has brought in a marketing consultant to help the firm reach the next level. This consultant has given her some blunt advice: "People are too comfortable here. Nobody wants to rock the boat. If you want new ideas, I think you'll have to bring in a lot of new people."

This advice goes against everything the CEO believes in. She values two-way loyalty and has always gone out of her way to hire strong managers and associates. She is sure the product teams are capable of developing innovations that could turn things around—but why so little result? Ellen calls in an old college friend, Sarah Hawthorne, recently retired from the corporate world and now operating independently, styling herself as "The Organizational Detective."

"Sarah," Ellen begins, "I want you to sit in on some of the product team meetings and see if you can find out why there are no really interesting ideas emerging. You don't have to name names, of course, but I'd like a report on what's getting in the way of better ideas."

"I can do that," Sarah replies, "but I'd also like to meet with the manager and the team members afterward, so I can understand the dynamics better."

A TYPICAL TEAM MEETING?

Sarah settles into her chair in the back of the room. The manager, Ephraim, is sitting in the front with six team members in chairs arranged in a semicircle facing him. Off to the side is a large screen, split, showing two remotely connected team members.

Ephraim starts the meeting by introducing Sarah. "She's here to spy on us today," he says with a grin. Sarah grimaces at the stale reference, then attempts to change it into a smile. She knows from experience that once the group gets started, she will become largely invisible.

Ephraim continues. "Our first item is to come up with some new ideas that we can bring to market quickly. Who has thought of something?" He pauses, looking to the group expectantly.

"Er . . . how about the new packaging idea I suggested last time?" a newer member of the team, Sascha, ventures.

"I don't think that will work, Sascha," says Spencer, the most senior member of the team and an informal leader. "I know you haven't been here that long, but we've tried that and learned that if the customers don't recognize us by our traditional brand features, we lose sales."

Silence for a long second, then Raj speaks. "What about offering three-packs?"

"Great idea, Raj!" Ephraim exclaims. Sarah knows that he has recently attended some management training sessions that emphasized positive feedback.

There is a lull. Then, from the group, several responses: "Yes, nice idea." "Good thinking, Raj."

"Any other ideas? . . . No? Karla and Sean, please get back to us next week with an analysis of costs and a proposal for pricing."

The team goes on to the next item. At the back of the room, Sarah jots down a few notes. The meeting ends right on time.

SARAH INVESTIGATES

Sarah is meeting with Ephraim. "How do you think the meeting went?" she asks.

"As usual, the team was pretty quiet," he replies. "I've tried to get them to engage more, but I think a lot of them are introverts. Fortunately, Raj has a lot of ideas and the others seem pretty supportive. I try to involve them in other ways, too."

"Are you satisfied with the current level of participation in problem-solving?"

"Not really. At least some of them are supposed to be pretty creative, based on their backgrounds—but they don't seem to show up that way in our meetings. I try to encourage them by praising the ideas they do come up with, but when they do speak up, it's more often to throw cold water on someone else's idea. I've asked them to be more positive, but I really don't know what else I can do with the current crew."

Sarah pauses, then comments, "So, at this point, you're feeling a bit stuck as to how to get them to offer more ideas."

Sarah plans to meet with the team members. She will tell them that she will keep their specific responses confidential but will put together a report with the general themes that arise from her interviews.

_____

"Sascha, how do you think the meeting went?" Sarah inquires.

"It was OK. Kind of what I've come to expect."

"Say more about that if you can," she persists.

"Sure. We all like Ephraim but the meetings are pretty boring. He'll ask for input on something, but somebody usually shoots down any idea that would amount to a real change. Then we all try to figure out what he really wants us to say and somebody, usually Raj, comes up with it and we can get back to work. I do try once in a while—you know, throw a pebble at the window just to see if anyone's home. But it soon gets tiresome, and I don't want to be seen as a troublemaker."

"What do you do if you don't like the idea that seems to be moving forward?"

"Think about who else is hiring . . . there's just not much of a reward for being critical. People take it personally and Ephraim doesn't like it—I can tell from his facial expressions. It's not worth it."

SARAH REPORTS TO ELLEN

"Ellen," Sarah begins, "I spoke with Ephraim and all of the team members. Several themes emerged, and the team members were quite consistent. They said they felt that Ephraim's questions were often 'pro forma'—that he had already decided on a solution or action and was just looking for someone in the group to come up with the same idea, which he then supported enthusiastically. At times when he didn't seem to have a pre-decided solution, he jumped on the first decent idea that emerged and sounded so positive about it that the rest of the team backed off, especially if they had an idea that was very different from what he appeared to be approving. A few of them also noted that people were always trying to read his mind and if they thought he didn't like a suggestion, they would react negatively to it. And almost all of them mentioned that the unspoken norm was avoidance of interpersonal conflict—so even the negative feedback was hedged and polite. At the same time, they all assured me that Ephraim was in other ways a good manager: thoughtful and supportive."

Ellen Madrigal thinks for a moment, then opens up. "He is that, and I'd like to see if we can help him. I know you're going to share this feedback summary with him later today. Can you give him some tips on how to help his team come up with better ideas?"

"I can and will. But I think there's a skill deficit on the team, as well. They don't seem to know how to persist without being confrontational. They back off quickly if they don't get Ephraim's immediate approval—and the conversation seems to have a 'starfish' quality: everything goes back and forth between Ephraim and the individual, and there's little or no general discussion or debate among the team members. So, there's no way that they can build on and improve one another's ideas. Would you be interested in having me work with the entire team to see if we can build a more robust process?"

"That works for me, Sarah. Let me know when you can start."

PART TWO

HOW TO BUILD
BETTER IDEAS

Learning the Skills of Constructive Debate

4 ■ Introduction to the Skills of Constructive Debate

In this section, we'll focus on a collaborative form of debate. The behavioral skills involved require some conscious intent and the process itself requires some structure. While the skills are relatively simple to learn, they are not just "doing what comes naturally" under the circumstances where they are most needed, and thus are not necessarily easy. They call for both positive intent and personal discipline. And these skills are more likely to be practiced in a culture or environment that supports the process and encourages the practices of constructive debate.

Constructive debaters will:

- Bring up a variety of ideas for consideration
- Encourage both creative and critical thinking
- Support collaborative exploration of problems and opportunities
- Confront difficult issues directly
- Focus on identifying and developing promising ideas

Any process that is designed to lead to a good decision needs to include both inquiry and advocacy.[8] *Inquiry* interrogates thoughts, suggestions, and proposals. *Advocacy* promotes specific ideas. Both processes are essential to building better, more-robust ideas and to good decision-making. So that we can debate in a constructive and productive way, we need to develop skills in the following four focus areas:

- *Expressing Ideas:* Offering a suggestion or proposal supported by relevant reasons or examples (advocacy)
- *Engaging Others:* Drawing colleagues into a discussion to take advantage of their thinking and test your own (inquiry)
- *Exploring Views:* Working collaboratively and interactively to test and develop ideas (inquiry and advocacy)
- *Challenging Positions:* Confronting potential problems that could cause difficulty in decision-making (inquiry and advocacy)

Within each of the focus areas, there are three skills, as shown in Figure 1.

Express Ideas

Expressing Ideas is the ability to offer a suggestion or proposal that is supported by relevant reasons or examples. Done well, this can encourage oneself and others to communicate ideas in a manner that leads to a rich variety of possible approaches. Done poorly, it can lead to loss of respect and to low-quality ideas.

Behaviors associated with Express Ideas include:

- **Make suggestions**
  Present an idea, opinion, or solution that is relevant to a specific topic or issue.
- **Offer reasons**
  Provide a rationale or data that supports a position, suggestion, opinion, or solution.

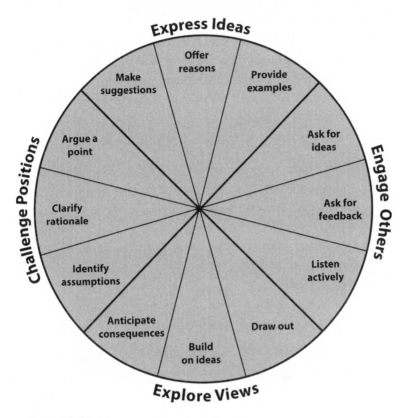

Figure 1: CD Model

- *Provide examples*
  Offer illustrations that demonstrate the value of a position, suggestion, or opinion.

These behaviors enable a group of people to place a variety of ideas on the table for consideration. Leaders can encourage team members to use these skills by making enough time in a meeting for new ideas to emerge, by not evaluating those ideas positively or negatively until later, by staying open to alternatives until many have been suggested, and by using processes that make it easy for everyone to contribute.

Engage Others

Engaging Others is the ability to draw colleagues into a discussion so as to take advantage of their thinking and test your own. Done well, this can lead to greater involvement as well as higher-quality ideas. Done poorly, it can lead to cynicism, loss of trust, and the withholding of useful feedback.

Behaviors associated with Engage Others include:

- *Ask for ideas*
  Address a question to a group or another person in order to solicit their ideas on a specific topic.
- *Ask for feedback*
  Solicit others' opinions about your own ideas, behavior, or action.
- *Listen actively*
  Paraphrase or summarize another person's position, idea, or feedback in a neutral, nonjudgmental way.

These behaviors encourage greater participation, begin the process of enriching ideas, invite objective evaluation of ideas, and discourage defensiveness. Leaders encourage these behaviors the most by modeling them.

Explore Views

Exploring Views means the ability to work collaboratively and interactively to test and develop ideas. Done well, this can lead to more advanced ideas and greater ownership of eventual decisions or solutions. Done poorly, it can lead to sloppy thinking and low support for decisions.

Behaviors associated with Explore Views include:

- *Draw out*
  Query others in a way that deepens or extends your understanding of the information, idea, or point of view they have offered.
- *Build on ideas*
  Add to, enhance, or elaborate on an idea offered by another.

- *Anticipate consequences*
  Pursue an idea to its logical conclusion.

These behaviors serve to deepen the quality of the conversation, promote greater collaboration, and open up a discussion to prevent unintended consequences. Leaders can normalize these behaviors by initiating them and openly appreciating the give-and-take.

Challenge Positions

Challenging Positions is the willingness and ability to confront potential problems that could cause difficulties along the road to decision and implementation. Done well, this can lead to mutual trust and respect within a team and the avoidance of preventable problems. Done poorly, it can lead to defensiveness and unproductive conflict.

Behaviors associated with Challenge Positions include:

- *Identify assumptions*
  Identify and question limiting assumptions associated with an opinion, solution, or position or encourage others to do so.
- *Clarify rationale*
  Ask another person or challenge yourself to provide logical support for an idea.
- *Argue a point*
  Disagree with another person or with "common wisdom" by providing an alternate rationale or data leading to a different conclusion.

These behaviors highlight flaws in ideas—not to make anyone wrong, but rather to let the group correct or improve the ideas before making any decisions. Again, the best way for leaders to promote these more-difficult behaviors is to model them—to be explicit in challenging their own ideas before inviting others to do the same.

While the four skill-sets are distinct, and each has its uses, they also represent roughly a sort of flow that should take place—usually with iterations—in any constructive debate. First you generate ideas, then you evaluate them, next you build on and improve them, and finally you put them through a test of strength. As you move from one "phase" of the debate to the next, you will take the time to narrow or filter the ideas, so that you can focus on moving the most promising of them forward. However, this is not a lockstep process. Often, when a new idea is introduced or when the process stalls, a leader, facilitator, or member should suggest returning to a previous phase, because to achieve the best outcome there needs to be a free flow both forward and back as the topic and process demand.

In the next few chapters, we'll take a closer look at these four skillsets and explore how to put them to work. In each of these chapters, you'll find a more detailed description of each of the skills, an example of how it might sound, and then some sentence-starters that can help you form a statement or question within that skill. Following that will be a set of criteria for using the skill effectively. You can use these criteria to prepare and also to provide feedback as appropriate.

A CONVERSATION WITH EPHRAIM

"As you know, Ephraim," Sarah begins, "I've just completed interviews with your team. I'll give you a summary of how they answered my questions, but before I do, is there anything you especially want me to focus on?"

"As I mentioned the last time," Ephraim replies, "I'd really like to know why they tend to be so quiet in meetings. It's like pulling teeth to get them to share an idea."

Sarah shares her summary with him. As she does so, she notices that Ephraim seems surprised. There is a long silence after she finishes. Finally, he takes a deep breath and begins to speak. "I'm kind of stunned by this. You're telling me that my behavior is causing the problem. I think that's bull . . . er-nonsense. They're adults. Why should they be afraid of what I might say or do?"

"It's complicated, Ephraim. Your team thinks a lot of you, and they want to be in your good graces. I know you don't intend to shut them down, but perhaps you haven't considered how much power you represent. And how much that is experienced by your team members. You have a very diverse group, and many of them are from backgrounds that are more authoritarian than is common in your corporate culture. I'm assuming that most of them haven't had much experience or gained much skill in debating an issue in a constructive way."

Ephraim thinks for a moment. "That's probably true. The one or two who usually speak up are not necessarily the ones who might have the most interesting ideas. That has bothered me. What do you think I should do?"

"I can definitely give you some suggestions about ways to encourage greater engagement. If you're open to it, Ellen suggested that we might do a training session on the skills that can help your team gain confidence in participating. But first, people on the team need to know that you're genuinely interested in a process of give-and-take, not just quick agreement."

"How can I communicate that to them in a believable way?"

"Let's plan a short team meeting where you can talk about what you hope the team can accomplish regarding the current issue and then discuss how to make the next meeting very open, creative, and maybe even exciting. We can establish some norms that will make it easier, and I'll help you plan it so that more people participate. If you demonstrate this consistently, people will come to trust that you really want to hear their ideas."

THE MEETING BEFORE THE MEETING

Team members arrive or join the meeting remotely on the large screen. Sarah notices a lot of shuffling and a buzz of conversation in the room. Ephraim starts the meeting with a question: "Hi, everybody. I've been thinking: What can we do to make our next meeting really creative? I'd like to be able to bring a lot of new and interesting ideas to the senior team. I've learned a lot from the feedback you gave to Sarah, and she's going to help me take a step back while you generate and develop a number of new ideas. I want you to know that I'm really open to a lot of different options. And I'd also like you to keep me honest about staying open and not making decisions too soon. What do you think are some 'rules of the road' that might help us do that?"

Sarah is standing by a whiteboard and making notes on it. "Don't judge ideas too early, either positively or negatively," she quickly writes. "Listen to one another. Build on one another's ideas. Challenge any assumptions you hear."

The list grows. There is clearly a lot more energy in the room than there was at the last meeting. Sarah encourages the team members to decide how to enforce the norms in a way that is light but clear. The team considers throwing paper airplanes, but in the end decides on just reminding one another by calling out the norm. Ephraim makes the point that he particularly wants to be called out if he oversteps. They agree on a set of norms for next week's meeting, in which they will focus once more on suggestions that will help the company differentiate itself and gain market share.

Afterward, Ephraim and Sarah develop a plan for the upcoming meeting. She wants to introduce the concept of "constructive debate" at the beginning, and Ephraim agrees to that.

5 ▪ Expressing Ideas

Most researchers and experts in innovation agree that having a greater number of ideas to choose from makes it more likely that you will end up with a higher-quality and more-innovative solution. As noted earlier, many such experts also suggest that diverse groups generate much more creative ideas. Diversity may be in age, gender, professional background, status, experience, ethnicity, and so on—all can contribute to a richer ideation session. (Teams with fluid boundaries might benefit from including "ad hoc" members for specific debates so they can gain the diversity they otherwise lack.) The skills we will explore in this chapter, shown in Figure 2, are designed to help individuals get a hearing, especially for new and unusual ideas.

Make Suggestions

When you make a suggestion, you are presenting an idea, opinion, or solution in relation to a specific topic or issue. Sometimes a

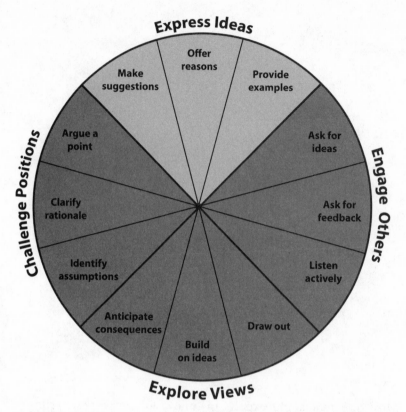

Figure 2: Express Ideas

suggestion is a response to a problem that has already been framed; other times, it is an initiative that takes the conversation in a new direction. Since the ultimate purpose of constructive debate is to develop promising ideas, a large number and a wide variety of suggestions should be encouraged early in the process. Suggestions should be made with as little personal attachment to them as possible; this attitude allows them to be reshaped, developed, or dropped, or perhaps to serve as a stimulus to other ideas.

Making suggestions that lie outside of what is considered one's turf or that go against the organization's common wisdom can require courage. True innovation often comes from using "beginner's mind" (the Zen Buddhist notion of *shoshin*—or approaching things openly and without preconceptions) or from moving beyond one's boundaries. Leaders and teams alike need to create a climate that encourages conscious, intelligent risk-taking so as to produce the large number of ideas that can allow a few truly great ones to emerge. We will discuss that climate in chapter 11.

Example:
"I suggest that we develop a version of that product that will be a better fit for the Latin American market."

Sentence-starters:
- *"Here's what I think about . . ."*
- *"I'd like to suggest . . ."*
- *"My solution would be . . ."*
- *"I propose . . ."*

Criteria:
To be most effective, suggestions should:

- Be stated clearly and unambiguously
- Be relevant to the issue at hand
- Be brief and to the point
- Be at a "big picture" level

Offer Reasons
When you offer reasons, you provide a rationale or data that supports a proposition, suggestion, opinion, or solution. You can begin with the reasons, then lead to the suggestion, or you can state your conclusion first, then support it with the reasons. Reasons can be based on objective, self-evident data, or on inferences that logically follow from evidence or a stated premise. To get your points across to as many listeners as possible and to increase the likelihood of their receptivity, select the reasons that are the strongest and most compelling, rather than offering a large number of reasons or only the ones that convinced you.

Reasons may be compelling because:

- They are exceptionally clear and easy to demonstrate
- They are especially relevant to the problem or issue
- They are particularly meaningful to the audience

A common error is to offer too many reasons. In a debate, this encourages others to focus on the weaker reasons rather than attending to those that are most solid. If the reasons are not self-evident (for example, "there are exactly three people on this team"), you will need to clarify or offer proof of the truth or relevance of the reason.

Example:
"I have three reasons for recommending this course of action. First, it is the least expensive; second, it offers the most flexibility; and third, we have the right resources within the team already. The resources I am referring to are . . ."

Sentence-starters:
- *"Here are the facts that convinced me . . ."*
- *"I think this will work because . . ."*
- *"Here are three reasons for . . ."*
- *"I reached this conclusion because . . ."*

Criteria:
To be most effective, reasons should:

- Be meaningful to those who receive them
- Strongly support your suggestion
- Be few in number and high in quality
- Be objective rather than subjective

Provide Examples
Examples demonstrate the value of a position, suggestion, or opinion. They bring a suggestion to life and can show others clearly how your suggestion relates to longer-term goals. The most useful reality-based examples are ones that involve shared experiences or commonly observed phenomena. Examples that illustrate and clarify a sugges-

tion can also be conjectural (understood as an educated guess) if they logically follow from accepted premises and can be shown to be clearly related to the suggestion.

Example:
"Let me tell you about a customer call I received yesterday . . ."

Sentence-starters:
- *"The result of taking this action is likely to be . . ."*
- *"One experience that convinced me was . . ."*
- *"If we did this, I believe that X would happen . . ."*
- *"Here's an example of how this would work . . ."*

Criteria:
To be most effective, examples should:

- Be connected to your suggestion
- Clarify your suggestion
- Be able to be demonstrated in some way
- Be believable, given the listeners' experience

When a team's energy is focused on generating ideas and the leader is able to keep the forum open and agnostic about position, tenure, or territory, the process can lead to the productive and positive development of a wide range of possibilities. This can lead to more-creative solutions, resolutions, and innovations.

The more skill a team has in expressing ideas, the more likely it is that they will generate a broad set of alternatives, increasing the likelihood that one or more of the ideas will prove to be promising. See the table titled "Criteria for Effectiveness" for suggestions on developing such skills.

THE FIRST IDEATION SESSION

Sarah describes the Constructive Debate process to Ephraim's team and explains the behavior model. She suggests that they practice Expressing Ideas in this session. First, she reviews the norms they had

Summary: Criteria for Effectiveness: Express Ideas

Make Suggestions	Offer Reasons	Provide Examples
To be most effective, suggestions should: • Be stated clearly and unambiguously • Be relevant to the issue at hand • Be brief and to the point • Be at a "big picture" level	To be most effective, reasons should: • Be as specific as possible • Strongly support your suggestion • Be few in number • Be objective rather than subjective	To be most effective, examples should: • Be connected to your suggestion • Clarify your suggestion • Be able to be demonstrated in some way • Be believable, given the listeners' experience

agreed on in the previous session and asks if they still agree or want to change or add anything.

Ephraim restates the problem they are to focus on. "What can we do to differentiate ourselves and increase our market share? I know you've had some time to think about it, so I'd like to do a 'round robin' brainstorming exercise. Everyone will share an idea or pass. We won't evaluate any of these ideas, either positively or negatively. Sarah will list them on the whiteboard. Let's permit the ideas to run down a couple of times before we stop. You might find that another person's idea will make a connection for you during the silences, and you'll come up with something new."

Ideas begin to flow, at first with hesitation and then more freely.

"Special limited-edition flavors for holidays."

"Mini-sizes for people on diets."

"Cultural themes—cultured cultures!"

"Spiced flavors."

"How about savory yogurts?"

"Kits for mixing yogurt with other ingredients to make salad dressing, sauces, or fancy desserts."

"Maybe we can create an alcoholic drink—a yogtail?"

Ideas continue to flow, then ebb, then crest again. Finally, after the second long silence, Ephraim calls time.

"I really like . . . Ephraim hesitates, blinks, then continues ". . . the number of ideas you came up with. Now let's choose a few that seem really promising."

Sarah facilitates a quick discussion about criteria for "promising ideas." The team agrees that the ideas should be new to the market, able to be manufactured largely with existing equipment, and require little change in branding or packaging.

Proponents of the ideas offer reasons or examples to promote their suggestion, showing how they match to the criteria. They choose several ideas, using a decision method where each person gets three votes and can use them for three different ideas or "spend" them on only one or two.

Five ideas have the preponderance of votes. Ephraim circles them on the whiteboard. "Next meeting, we'll have some give-and-take about these ideas. Sarah will give us a tutorial on what she calls 'Engaging Others.'"

"I almost blew it, didn't I?" Ephraim asked Sarah as they did a post-meeting review. "I do like one of the ideas a lot—but I won't even tell you which one it is. I caught myself before I blurted that out. I've been so used to praising people for specific ideas instead of for a good process. And I know I would have stopped it before we even got to that idea if you hadn't given me the feedback about how I was cutting off the team's creative thinking."

6 ■ Engaging Others

A colleague of mine once humorously requested, "Give me some feedback, but don't get any on me!" I thought that her comment was, though intended as a joke, a perfect description of the attitude of many participants in meetings I have observed as an organizational consultant. And I can understand why. I have observed that people often feel extremely attached to some of their ideas, and present them with the assumption that others will appreciate their value, only to be shocked and even hurt by negative comments. On the other hand, many participants in such meetings are not highly skillful in providing feedback or upgrades to other people's ideas and may come across as attacking the person rather than criticizing the idea. Unacknowledged or open competitiveness can also affect the tenor of comments and make it less likely that colleagues would want to put themselves in the position of approving of, or improving, the ideas of people they consider rivals. The result can be an attack/defend spiral that is based on emotion rather than rea-

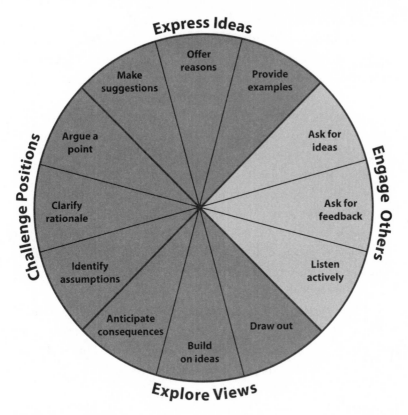

Figure 3: Engage Others

son and wastes time that could be better spent developing robust solutions.

A culture and a set of norms that encourage collaboration can lead not only to a better work environment, but also to stronger ideas that are owned by the many rather than fought for by the individual. The skills we discuss in this chapter, shown in Figure 3, encourage engagement and invite participants in a constructive debate to experience curiosity rather than defensiveness.

Ask for Ideas
When you ask for ideas, you address a question to another person so you can solicit their ideas on a specific topic. It's easy to assume,

especially if you are from a Western culture, that if a team member has an idea, he or she will contribute it. This assumption, however, ignores the realities of a diverse workforce. Differences in personality, culture, role, or status may all affect a person's willingness or ability to take initiative in bringing an idea or opinion to the table. If only the most extroverted or senior members of the team speak up, important information and innovative ideas may be lost.

As a leader or team member, you show respect for others and take advantage of their thinking by engaging them directly in the discussion. This is especially important for global teams, whose meetings often take place via teleconference, making it easy for more introverted or lower-ranking members to be ignored. Instead, you can initiate processes that make it easy and important to hear ideas from all members (see appendix 1, "Skills and Tools for Facilitating a Constructive Debate").

In the long run, *all of us are smarter than any one of us*—and team members are more likely to be aligned and committed to an eventual decision or outcome when they have participated in the discussions and debates leading up to that result.

Example:
"How do you think we ought to approach this problem?"

Sentence-starters:
- *What do you think about . . . ?"*
- *"I'd like to know your opinion about . . ."*
- *"I'd like to hear some different alternatives for . . ."*
- *"I'd be interested in your thoughts on this, [name] . . ."*

Criteria:
To be most effective, the question should:

- Be open-ended
- Be stated in a neutral, non-judgmental way
- Stimulate others' thinking
- Encourage a group or a specific individual to speak

Ask for Feedback

Asking for feedback means actively soliciting another person's opinion about your own ideas, behavior, or action. This is difficult for many of us. Often we prefer to assume that others agree with us, unless they volunteer another point of view. We can feel highly vulnerable whenever we ask others to critique our ideas. As a result, many ideas get critiqued out of the hearing of those who would have the most to learn and benefit from the feedback. And if a team or organization is serious about the quality of its ideas, there is no substitute for a climate of open feedback.

The key to effectiveness in the use of this behavior is a willingness to hear disconfirming feedback. If you ask for feedback and then respond in an angry or defensive manner, you will not be taken seriously the next time. Asking for and receiving feedback with an attitude of curiosity, interest, and openness to improving the idea makes it more likely that the ideas that emerge from a constructive debate will be of higher quality. Thanking the sender and asking for more information or clarification will encourage a constructive exchange.

Example:
"You've all heard my proposal. Tell me what you think about it—what works well and what I need to modify."

Sentence-starters:
- *"I'd like your reaction to my proposal . . ."*
- *"What holes do you see in my logic?"*
- *"What did you think about the way I approached that?"*
- *"What could I have done better?"*

Criteria:
To be most effective, the request for feedback should:

- Be neutral in tone, not sarcastic or threatening
- Be followed by a silence indicating readiness to listen
- Encourage the other to disagree or offer course corrections
- Be made early and often

Listen Actively

Active listening means paraphrasing or summarizing another person's position, idea, or feedback in a neutral, non-judgmental way. You will use this skill to make sure you have understood another person's feedback or idea clearly before you respond to it. It's also possible that the other person will offer a correction or adjustment of the statement in order to clarify it, to prevent misrepresentation, or even to improve the idea after hearing it paraphrased.

Active listening is a valuable skill to use—and also to ask others to use—under circumstances where conflicting interests and ideas are creating an unproductive climate in a group. Careful listening provides time to reflect on the value of a thought or idea before reacting to it; it requires you to focus on the other's position rather than thinking of a retort or practicing one-upmanship. Active listening does not suggest either agreement or disagreement; its purpose is to foster deliberation and mutual respect.

Example:
"So your preference would be to get several quotes rather than to single-source it."

Sentence-starters:
- *"So, from your point of view . . ."*
- *"Your position is . . ."*
- *"Where you disagree with this proposal is . . . . Do I have that right?"*
- *"So you think I should have . . ."*

Criteria:
To be most effective, the listening behavior should:

- Be a fair restating of the other's view
- Be relatively brief and focused on key points
- Lack any information about your own opinion
- Be followed by a "quizzical" silence or a question, to test whether you have fully understood

A variant of this listening behavior that we often use when teaching innovation management is a process called "Dragons' Den," in which small groups present an innovative idea to the class and then invite feedback from other participants (the fierce "dragons" in the den) in the form of challenging questions such as *"What if. . . ?" "Have you considered . . . ?" "How would you . . . ?"* The group must respond simply with thanks—no explanations or clarifications allowed, though they are encouraged to take notes. After all have presented, the small groups meet and consider how to use the feedback to improve their idea or their presentation. They then share with the rest of the participants how they used the feedback. Often, organizations that adopt this as a regular practice report that it increases support for unusual ideas, especially among key stakeholders.

This skill-set is intended to help meeting participants replace defensiveness with curiosity—to invite critiques rather than repel

Summary: Criteria for Engaging Others

Ask for Ideas	Ask for Feedback	Listen Actively
To be most effective, the question should:	To be most effective, the request for feedback should:	To be most effective, the listening behavior should:
• Be open-ended	• Be neutral in tone, not sarcastic or threatening	• Be a fair restating of the other's view
• Be stated in a neutral, non-judgmental way	• Be followed by a silence indicating readiness to listen	• Be relatively brief and focused on key points
• Stimulate others' thinking	• Encourage the other to disagree or offer course corrections	• Lack any information about your own opinion
• Encourage a group or specific individual to speak	• Be made early and often	• Be followed by a "quizzical" silence or a question to test whether you have understood

them, based on the attitude and useful assumption that others can help you to improve your idea. By inviting both positive and negative comments, this skill-set reduces the sting of unexpected negative feedback, reinterpreting it as a positive contribution. This approach may also influence others, through engaging with an idea, to come on board and help move it forward. See the table "Summary: Criteria for Engaging Others" for strategies to help you develop a broad skill-set.

IMPROVING THE IDEAS

"So," Sarah comments, summarizing her presentation, "one of the most effective ways to build better ideas is to get other people engaged in improving yours. Why do you think we hesitate to do that a lot of the time?" She pauses. The team members shift in their chairs. The silence becomes uncomfortable enough for someone to break it. Jason and Susan start to speak at the same time.

"We might not like what other people think about our ideas." "We might get defensive."

Sascha adds, "We might not like to be criticized in front of the boss."

Sarah drills down on the team. "How do you feel about giving feedback to one another—about what you like and don't like about a suggestion?"

"In my experience," says Raj, "people might say they want feedback, but they really don't. They want agreement or praise."

"I don't want to create conflict, so I usually just hope the bad ideas die a natural death," Sascha adds, with a wry grin.

"Let's try something different today," Sarah replies. "I'll ask the people who are championing each of the five ideas you chose in the last meeting to invite feedback, both positive and negative." She turns to the five people representing the ideas. "When you hear it, you can ask for more information about what the other person is thinking, or you can use active listening to summarize what they said. But don't agree or disagree. Don't explain. For now, just stay neutral. Turn off your natural urge to defend, and turn on your curiosity instead. And I'd like each of you, after the feedback session, to tell us what that experience was like."

FEEDBACK AND RESPONSES

Susan's idea is the final one to be put forward for the team's critique. They will ask her some challenging questions based on what they think needs to be corrected, improved, or strengthened.

"I think we should manufacture yogurts that are savory," Susan begins. "The natural flavor of yogurt is a bit sour and tangy, so why not build on that rather than disguise it with sugar? We could have flavors like sun-dried tomato, bacon, artichoke, smoked salmon and dill, or blue cheese. They could be used as sauces or dressings as well as eaten on their own—they could even be the base of appetizers for lunch or dinner rather than being confined to breakfast."

Sarah encourages the group to challenge Susan and reminds her that she is not to defend or explain, but simply to thank each person for the feedback.

Raj speaks up. "Have you considered how difficult it will be to get people to try something that goes against their experience and expectations?"

"Thank you," Susan says.

Others join the fray. "What if the machines that we currently use can't process this new set of ingredients?"

"Thanks."

"Have you made a cost estimate of this innovation and how it might affect pricing?"

"Thank you."

The questions continue. Susan seems to find it easier as the process goes on. Eventually, the team runs down.

Sarah asks each of the people who posed an idea to describe their responses to the "Dragons' Den" experience.

One offers, "It was freeing not to have to defend my idea—I was able to really listen to the feedback."

Another suggests, "I could see the holes in my idea and I didn't have to feel embarrassed by that—I felt like the others were really assisting me."

"It was nice to see how I could improve my presentation before I have to give it to the decision-makers!"

"At first, I felt a little defensive and wanted to explain, but after a couple of the questions, I relaxed and just took it in. I think saying 'thank you' reminded me that they were really trying to help me improve my idea."

Sarah smiles, pauses for a few moments, and wraps up the discussion by saying, "So, this is one tool you might want to use to 'engage others' in building and improving your idea." The entire team nods in agreement. The meeting is over.

7 ■ Exploring Views

To explore views means to go more deeply into what team members express when asked for ideas. Too many ideas in business today receive a shallow review and are moved forward because of the pressure of time, an over-focus on results, discomfort with process, or because people don't believe they are really going to have any influence on important decisions. Once ideas have been aired, and exposed to both positive and negative feedback, it's time for some critical thinking. You can't think critically about an idea you don't fully comprehend, so it's important to learn more about an idea under consideration before you can begin to develop and improve it. This part of the debate is where the rough edges of an idea that showed up in negative feedback are shaved off and the positive interior structure is strengthened. See key terms in Figure 4.

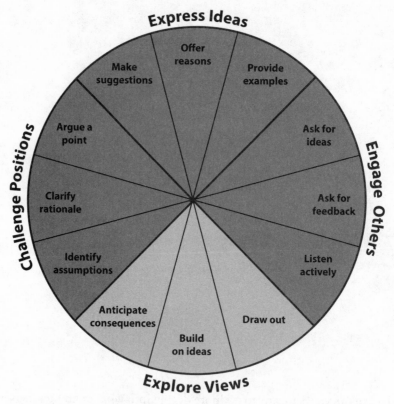

Figure 4: Explore Views

Draw Out

When you draw out, you query others in a way that deepens or extends your understanding of the information, idea, or point of view they have offered. Listening actively is a good start, but to further your understanding and establish conditions for developing the idea, you will need to go beyond your initial "take" on the idea and drill down to discover more. Using this skill stimulates others to be more thoughtful in the way they present their ideas and to communicate more fully and directly. The knowledge that someone is listening carefully and has enough interest to follow up generally improves the quality of the dialogue and may even improve the quality of the thought behind it. The goal of this approach is to begin a joint exploration of the idea or proposal; it is *not* to make the other person wrong or to put her or him on the spot. This should stimulate a broader discussion by the team. It's also an opportunity to demonstrate that a variety of alternatives can be explored in a fair and nonthreatening way, thereby encouraging the expression of innovative ideas.

Example:
"Please say more about the reaction you expect from the vendors."

Sentence-starters:
- *"Help me understand your idea about . . ."*
- *"What would be an example of that?"*
- *"How would you see that working in . . ."*
- *"Tell me more about . . ."*

Criteria:
To be most effective, drawing out should:

- Be based on something the other has actually said or implied
- Invite the other to offer reasons or examples
- Inspire the other to extend their thinking on the topic
- Not reveal one's own judgment or opinion

When a person offers an idea, it's possible that it just then occurred to them, but often the idea is one that's been in the oven for a while. So, before you go further and explore it, it's best to learn how long they have been thinking about it, what options they have considered for improving on it, and what new thoughts have been developing based on the feedback they have received. You can find out how strongly they feel about various aspects of the idea and where they have the most flexibility. Most important, you can make sure that everyone has a chance to be clear about it before you begin to develop it further.

Build on Ideas
This behavior allows you to add to, enhance, or elaborate on an idea offered by others. It encourages team members to share ideas that

are still in development, which can lead to joint ownership and broader support. "Constructive Debate," as suggested by its name, focuses on the building and improving of ideas, not on tearing them apart. Making an idea stronger, more supportable, more applicable, or more innovative is an activity that can involve many minds. In an atmosphere where only individual work is recognized and rewarded, people may hold back from improving the ideas of others, hoping instead to compete successfully with those ideas. Unfortunately, too many organizations subvert the idea-building process by failing to provide team rewards and recognition.

Trust is a strong requirement for sharing and building on ideas. You have to trust that others will not take credit inappropriately or discount your idea by discussing it with others outside the team. A practical set of norms that sets out how the team wants ideas to be treated will help establish this trust.

Example:
"I'd like to build on that suggestion by opening the session up to a wider range of participants; let's invite people from the regions to send representatives."

Sentence-starters:
- *"I'd like to build on your suggestion by . . ."*
- *"Yes, and what if we . . ."*
- *"Going further along that line, how about . . ."*
- *"Let's expand on that idea . . ."*

Criteria:
To be most effective, when building ideas, you should:
- Be accurate in your characterization of the other's idea
- Acknowledge the other's contribution
- Expand the idea along the same or a similar line of thought
- Make the original idea more innovative or powerful

If a team is working on an important solution or opportunity, it's especially important that everyone be given a chance to contribute to it, so that they will be more likely to feel committed to selling or implementing the final result.

Anticipate Consequences

Pursuing an idea to its logical conclusion can help to enlarge or deepen the discussion. Too often in today's business world, we take an idea at face value and either accept or reject it without exploring further. This may cause us to lose a valuable line of inquiry that may be put forth in a tentative or ineffective way. Sometimes the most far-out idea can take us in an interesting new direction . . . if someone is willing to pursue it.

An important application of this skill is to help a group think about the possible unintended consequences of a decision or action. Hasty decisions can lead to costly and disastrous outcomes. The process of exploring ideas before accepting or rejecting them can be time-consuming, so people tend to rush through it—but when we do, the usual result is that we fall back on common wisdom and the politically correct ideas of the day. A commitment to follow more-unusual ideas through to conclusion is likely to lead to real change and innovation.

Example:
"This is a different line of thought from those we have been exploring. Let's follow it through and see where it leads us. What might be the result of taking that action?"

Sentence-starters:
- *"What are the implications of that idea?"*
- *"Where would that take us?"*
- *"What would logically follow from that?"*
- *"Let's continue this line of thinking by . . ."*

Criteria:

To be most effective, anticipating consequences should:

- Extend the idea to a logical endpoint
- Invite the other or the group to think together
- Go beyond the obvious, not be satisfied with pat answers
- Highlight potentially negative outcomes in a neutral way

These behaviors enlist the entire group or team in deepening ideas and can help to prevent unanticipated, undesired consequences. As individuals, we can be both blind to flaws in our own thinking and overly optimistic about outcomes if our suggestions should win the day. By temporarily setting aside our ownership of an idea and inviting colleagues to explore, we gain the power of collective intelligence—sometimes called the "hive mind" (think of the collective power of a beehive)—to improve our proposals and solutions. See the table "Summary: Criteria for Exploring Views" for strategies to develop exploration skills.

Summary: Criteria for Exploring Views

Draw Out	Build on Ideas	Anticipate Consequences
To be most effective, drawing out should:	To be most effective, building on ideas should:	To be most effective, anticipating consequences should:
• Be based on something the other has actually said or clearly implied	• Be accurate in its characterization of the other's idea	• Extend the idea to a logical end point
• Invite the other to offer reasons or examples	• Acknowledge the other's contribution	• Invite the other or the group to think together
• Invite the other to extend their thinking on the topic	• Expand the idea along the same or a similar line of thought	• Go beyond the obvious, not simply be satisfied with pat answers
• Not reveal one's own judgment or opinion	• Make the original idea more innovative or powerful	• Highlight potentially negative outcomes in a neutral way

TAKING THE NEXT STEP

As the next team meeting is about to begin, the room buzzes with conversation and excitement. The noise fades as Sarah Hawthorne walks in.

"Today, you're going to explore the ideas as deeply as you can," she begins. "I want you to learn more about each of the suggestions by drawing out the person who's championing it. Ask neutral, open-ended questions this time to develop a deeper understanding—this might also help the other person extend their thinking about the idea. Once you've done that, you can start to build on and improve the idea. And then, before we move on to the next one, think it through to what the possible consequences—whether positive or negative—could be. I'll facilitate, so you can focus on each idea. Our goal should be to end up with stronger, more-robust ideas by the end of our session. And you may even decide to leave a few of them behind."

A lively session ensues; the idea owners respond thoughtfully to questions—many of them pointing out areas they hadn't considered. The team members especially seem to enjoy coming up with wittily exaggerated "worst-case" scenarios about unintended consequences. It's fun and liberating, but the process also finds weak spots or risks that can be mitigated.

Finally, Sarah summarizes: "So I sense that you're interested in moving two ideas forward: The savory yogurts, and the 'cultural cultures.' Do I have that right?"

"Yes," offers Jason. "The other ones didn't really pass the test when we anticipated the consequences. The limited-edition ones might leave us with a lot of unusable inventory. The mini-sized ones seem as if the packaging would make them too expensive—the easier and less expensive solution would be to eat half at a time."

Susan speaks next. "I really appreciated all the new flavor ideas that people came up with. I'm pretty sure the savory yogurt idea is a winner!"

Raj adds, "And I liked having people ask me questions—it really pushed me to think through and develop my 'cultural' idea."

Sarah summarizes: "So it seems you're all pretty happy with where you are right now—the next time we meet, we're going to put that confidence to a test!"

8 ■ Challenging Positions

The ability to challenge someone's position without initiating interpersonal conflict is an art rather than a science. A neutral tone of voice and the communication of positive intention can nullify what might otherwise be taken as a personal attack. It's difficult, but essential, if you want to stop mediocre ideas from moving forward, to find a way to legitimize a focus on identifying and improving the weaker elements of an idea before it becomes the default solution. See Figure 5 for key concepts explored in this chapter.

Identify Assumptions
Unconscious assumptions are the enemy of critical thinking and constructive debate. If you're not aware of how you're limiting your thinking, you can't move beyond those limitations. You identify assumptions when you encourage another person—or even yourself!—

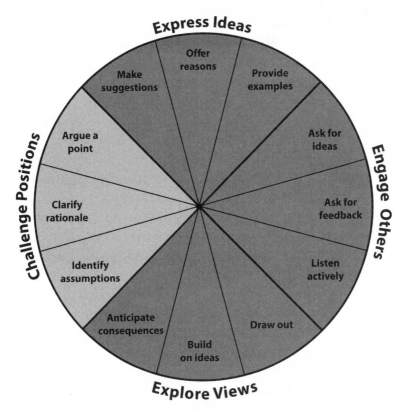

Figure 5: Challenge Positions

to observe and question any limiting assumptions associated with an opinion, solution, or position.

One key to success in critical thinking and constructive debate is the ability to take a temporarily neutral stance toward your own assumptions—even the most cherished ones. This enables you to test their:

- Basis in fact as opposed to opinions, values, habits, or vested interests
- Limiting effect on your thinking—what solutions or opportunities are you not considering as a result of your limiting assumptions?

Vested interests (what you have to gain or lose) frequently influence thinking and decision-making and can lead to faulty assumptions. It's important that you bring those interests into your conscious awareness so as not to fall into the trap of "wishful thinking." This trap awaits those who assume that the path that would produce the best outcome for them is also the most intelligent and strategic choice. Of course, vested interests are not always tangible gains or losses—for instance, the originator or champion of a previously chosen idea may fear a loss of respect or a reflection on their judgment if their idea is shot down by the group. These more emotional or psychological vested interests may not be as obvious and should, of course, be treated with some delicacy. Nevertheless, the assumptions that result can, and should, be questioned. And you may not want to be all that delicate with yourself!

Uncovering assumptions ought to be one of the aims of any constructive debate. Once you're aware of your assumptions, you can test them against what you and others know to be fact. This can move the conversation in a productive direction. This lets you abandon ideas based on faulty assumptions. It lets you identify issues over which you have control or influence and those that are outside your direct control or influence but that will have an impact on the outcome you are working toward. This may encourage you to do some important scenario planning that can lead you to strengthen your ideas.[9]

Most of the assumptions that guide our day-to-day behavior and decisions exist below our awareness. A good time to question those assumptions is when we are tackling problems or opportunities, especially if "common wisdom" is not achieving the results we are looking for.

Several specific areas are often rich in unexamined assumptions. They include:

- The definition of a problem or opportunity
- The cause of a problem
- Where the solution can be found
- How to approach an opportunity

- Your own ability to influence the course of events regarding the problem or opportunity

Example:
"We haven't come up with many solutions to this problem; I wonder if we're framing the problem too narrowly? How might we be limiting our thinking?"

Sentence-starters:
- *"What must we be assuming here?"*
- *"How are we limiting ourselves?"*
- *"How do you know that to be true?"*
- *"What would you suggest if we didn't assume that?"*

Criteria:
To be most effective, identifying assumptions should:

- Demonstrate willingness to examine and acknowledge one's own assumptions as well as others'
- Offer rigorous questioning of "common wisdom"
- Search for the factual basis behind statements
- Encourage exploring alternatives outside of current limits

Clarify Rationale
You clarify a rationale by asking another person, or even yourself, to provide logical support for an idea. When someone presents a position that doesn't seem to be supported by data, logic, or examples, it can be helpful to challenge the person to think through their rationale. This works best in an atmosphere characterized both by high trust and high challenge. Leaders can best stimulate this behavior in others by responding to questions about their own logic and conclusions in a frank, public way. It's especially useful when a leader or respected contributor first acknowledges the usefulness of the question and then expresses appreciation for the challenge. To be

successful, of course, a challenge must be perceived as helpful rather than as an attack.

Defensiveness is the enemy of reason. Defensiveness is less about the quality of someone's personality (though it is often blamed on that) and more about the quality of the dialogue that is encouraged in a group or team. When people feel that they must defend or justify even a badly thought-out position, that team has issues that go deeper than simple competitiveness. Competitiveness (of an idea) should be an outcome of constructive debate and be focused outwardly, rather than be used as a means to limit the challenging of ideas and thus their improvement.

Ideally, when you help another person to clarify their rationale, you will be perceived as participating in a collaborative process to build better, stronger, more-robust ideas.

Example:
"Help me follow the path that led you to that opinion."

Sentence-starters:
- *"What is your opinion based on?"*
- *"Tell me how you reached that conclusion."*
- *"That's an interesting point. Explain the logic to me."*
- *"Help me follow your argument."*

Criteria:
To be most effective, clarifying should:

- Be neutrally phrased
- Suggest implicitly or explicitly that the other's point may indeed be supportable
- Invite the other to develop ideas further
- Use silence after the statement to enable the other to think and then respond

Argue a Point

When you argue a point, you disagree with another person or with a generally accepted point of view by providing an alternate rationale leading to a different conclusion. As stated—correctly!—in "The Argument Clinic," a sketch by the hilarious 20th century comedy group Monty Python (if you missed them back then, do yourself a favor and check them out via the internet), an argument is "a connected series of statements intended to establish a definite proposition . . . an intellectual process . . . contradiction is just the automatic gainsaying of anything the other person says." In other words, an argument requires both thoughtful development and a willingness to share the rational process by which you came to a different conclusion, rather than merely an assertion that the other's position is clearly wrong.

You don't have to wait for others to put an argument forward in order to use this skill. A time-honored technique for persuasion is to raise a point that you believe others favor and then proceed to refute it in a thoughtful, rational manner.

Constructive debate is most likely to occur when the points being argued are ones that can be proven or supported through objective means, rather than by representing opinions based on faith or cherished values.

Example:

"Given the data we are using, I came to a different understanding of the problem. I believe that the factor that requires the most attention is our decision-making process. I'd like to show you, using this chart, where there are several redundant loops in it that add little or no value."

Sentence-starters:

- *"Here's another way to look at it . . ."*
- *"I reached a different conclusion—and here's why . . ."*
- *"I'd like you to consider this alternative, because . . ."*
- *"I disagree with that conclusion, based on . . ."*

Criteria:

To be most effective, an argument should:

- Focus on objective data where possible
- Emphasize "upselling" your position more than criticizing or downgrading the other's
- Have a clear rationale
- Not contain any evaluation of the other's intelligence, intention, or motivation

Although we don't always see it that way, it's a real gift to receive a challenge to our thinking—one that provokes us to reconsider conclusions; to come up with a better rationale, evidence, or examples;

Summary: Criteria for Challenging Positions

Identify Assumptions	Clarify Rationale	Argue a Point
To be most effective, identifying assumptions should:	To be most effective, clarifying should:	To be most effective, an argument should:
• Demonstrate willingness to examine and acknowledge one's own assumptions as well as others'	• Be neutrally phrased	• Focus on objective data where possible
• Offer rigorous questioning of "common wisdom"	• Suggest implicitly or explicitly that the other's point may be supportable	• Emphasize "upselling" your position more than criticizing the other's
• Search for the factual basis behind statements	• Invite the other to develop ideas further	• Have a clear rationale
• Encourage exploring alternatives outside current limits	• Use silence after the statement to enable the other to think and respond	• Not contain any evaluation of the other's intelligence, intention, or motivation

or simply to find a clearer way to communicate our ideas. Providing a practical, friendly process for this can lead to a significant improvement in the quality of ideas and solutions, and ultimately to greater success for the team or organization. See the table "Criteria for Challenging Positions" for strategies to challenge long-held positions.

THE REFINER'S FIRE

This morning is the last meeting in the series of sessions that Sarah has facilitated. She addresses her first comment to the team leader. "Ephraim, once we walk out of here today, I believe you'll have one or more strong and promising ideas that you can have your team prototype and present to the stakeholders. They've come a long way."

"Yes," he replies. "I never would have believed that they could be so creative and also so rigorous. And that they would take risks in confronting one another's thinking and then turn around and be great supporters."

Sarah nods, and adds, "Today will be strenuous exercise, though. Up to now, they've focused more on the ideas. In this session, things will get more personal."

Sarah begins the morning with a summary and a call to action. "Susan and Raj, your ideas will be the focus today. For the rest of the team: your role is to smooth away the rough edges of their ideas and refine them. You'll do this very directly, using the skills of 'Challenging Positions.' I'd like you to approach this in a very conscious, open way and to apply the skills to your own thinking as well as to theirs. Susan and Raj, I'd like you to follow the practice once again of listening—but this time, listen actively so the others know you have understood. Summarize their points as accurately as possible. You're then free to respond by clarifying your rationale, identifying any assumptions that you have or that you think they do—or simply using good data and logic to argue for your point of view."

"So, we can defend without being defensive?" Raj inquires.

"That's the idea. And I'll call for a summary and sense of agreement once you feel complete on each idea. Of course, you can all feel free to use any of the other skills we've practiced—for example, you might anticipate another consequence, draw the champion out, or provide a new example."

One of the team members addresses Raj. "You seem to be assuming that everyone lives or works in a multicultural environment. If they don't, won't some of your flavor suggestions seem too strange? I mean, we do a lot of business in the U.S. Midwest—harissa could be a bit overwhelming there."

"So, you think the flavors I'm suggesting might be too spicy to appeal to a lot of our customers."

"Yes, I do."

"My data show that Thai, Indian, and Mexican restaurants are as popular in those areas as they are on the coasts. So I think we can build on that familiarity."

Karla nods. "I guess you're right. I was thinking about my Minnesota childhood when horseradish was as hot as things got!"

Sascha adds, "Just a thought: let's use a symbol on the packaging to show how hot and spicy that flavor is."

Sarah is busy making notes of suggestions on a flipchart page. She plans to bring them up when she summarizes to see if the team will move forward with the main idea.

The discussion winds down and Susan is now on the "hot seat."

"Before you start," Susan begins, "I just want to acknowledge that I'm thinking that savory yogurt is a fairly new idea. I did research it, and there doesn't seem to be much on the market, so I'm assuming that it hasn't been tried in a major way and then failed."

"That was going to be my challenge, Susan. But here's another: How do you know that people will accept a major change in the way they categorize yogurt? If it's not for breakfast, will they know what to do with it?"

"Good point, Jason. We'll have to work with Marketing to develop a lead-up that will make it seem really cool. And also to tap into consumers' creativity—maybe we could have a contest?"

Toward the end of the meeting, Susan and Raj form subteams to help them develop prototypes to demonstrate their ideas. The meeting ends on a note of excitement and anticipation for the next steps.

The meeting room, with its large remote monitor, is very quiet after the team has left.

Sarah thinks for a moment, then says: "They seem very enthusiastic about both ideas, Ephraim. Once the prototypes are ready, I think your stakeholders—execs, department heads, and key customers—will be surprised and delighted!"

"Yes, these are really promising and, by now, well-developed. I think Ellen [the Madrigal Company's CEO] will be especially pleased."

"We do need to prepare the team for the inevitable critique from her and the other execs."

"You know, Sarah, they seem to be ready and looking forward to that. The skills we've been practicing will help them come across as both confident and open. We really did build some better ideas! Thanks, and I think we're ready to go ahead on our own."

"Always happy to be 'fired' for a good reason, Ephraim. I've outlived my usefulness—and that's a good thing!"

THE END OF THE BEGINNING

"They did a stunning presentation, Sarah." Ellen is speaking with her consultant in the quiet of the executive suite. "The prototypes were, frankly, delicious—well, except for the one with bacon and cilantro! I had to educate them that there is a small percentage of genetically unfortunate people—I'm one—to whom cilantro tastes like soap. But everything else was a winner, and I think both Susan's and Raj's ideas will be moving forward. And I was really impressed with the team's confidence and ability to handle questions and to critique themselves. This worked really well, Sarah, and I'll be in touch soon to talk about how we can build on it—especially what I can do to lead a 'culture' change. That's a funny word, now that I think of it! I guess we can look at the whole experience as a kind of 'fermentation' process, like making yogurt?"

Sarah, never one to ignore a bad pun, agrees that they have indeed begun a flavorful "culture-culture" change. "It's been a good journey, Ellen. I'm looking forward to seeing the new products in my local supermarket. It's been great working with you and your team."

PART THREE

DESIGNING FOR BETTER IDEAS

Implementing Constructive Debate

9 ■ Establishing the Conditions for Constructive Debate

Constructive debates are, for many, a new way to approach idea development and problem-solving. The process goes against some habitual patterns of interaction and may even challenge organizational taboos such as "don't contradict the boss" or "avoid the appearance of conflict in the team." To make the process successful, you'll want to make it easier for team members to accept the risks involved in speaking out and speaking up. This requires conscious and thoughtful design so you can reduce the risks of saying what you really think and make it easier and more rewarding to participate.

Risk, Trust, and Courage

We don't tend to take risks under conditions where we don't trust others to support us. Support doesn't have to mean agreement—it can actually take the form of listening with interest and curiosity before evaluating one's ideas. If even a single person takes the risk of challenging common wisdom and the roof doesn't fall in, it becomes easier for others to do so. When a leader or team encourages boundary-breaking ideas and then the team members work together to strengthen and refine them, it's less likely that they will hold back or edit their ideas before expressing them. If there is a lack of trust in a group, people will be cautious rather than courageous in participating in a lively exchange of ideas. But the ground has to be prepared, so it's wise to be explicit in explaining the purpose, norms, process, and expected results of this approach.

Preparing the Ground

As stated earlier, a constructive debate requires that participants have:

- Ability to communicate
- Open-mindedness
- A minimum of conflicting vested interests
- Shared values
- Compelling issues
- A clear and effective process

Ability to Communicate

Communication means moving thoughts and ideas from one mind to another. Clearly, no meaningful debate happens without it. Communication happens in two basic directions; both need to be operational so that meaning can be transferred:

- *Receptive communication:* the ability to draw information and ideas from others; to listen and to understand
- *Expressive communication:* the ability to frame information and ideas in a way that can be interpreted clearly and correctly by others

Communication can be hampered by several factors:

- Skill deficits
- Cultural or language differences

- The use of "jargon"
- Emotional barriers
- Interpersonal conflict
- Low trust in the group

Ensuring that all participants possess a good, basic set of communication skills or the support they need to overcome barriers will promote healthy and productive debate.

Open-Mindedness

No debate can be constructive in the way we have defined it when the participants operate from fixed positions. In formal debate, the rules require that participants take one side of an issue and speak from that position. The result is a contest in which proponents of each side become more and more fixed in their positions, while using intellectual energy to defend and attack. This can be an interesting and entertaining event, yet it does not generally lead to movement, agreement, or development of the best or most innovative ideas.

Leaders and teams can take the following actions to ensure that debates are conducted under the most open conditions possible:

- Establish and enforce a set of norms that require participants to listen actively to one another's point of view. (See "Norm-Setting" in appendix 3.)
- Separate the generating of ideas from development and decision-making. (See "Diffusion/Integration Rule" in appendix 3.)
- From time to time, use techniques that require participants to "switch sides" and explore the merits of others' opinions and ideas. (See "Creative Controversy" in appendix 3.)
- Encourage asking for and giving constructive feedback on ideas and proposals.

In addition, consider issues of rank and power and how they may prevent "politically incorrect" ideas from being brought up, or discourage people from raising issues, or stand in the way of their getting a fair hearing. If you believe this is happening, discuss this in your team or with specific individuals and consider how to deal with it. Some possible actions include soliciting statements and demonstrations from more senior members, using anonymous techniques to poll the group, or setting up subgroups to generate and suggest ideas.

Minimum of Conflicting Vested Interests

Vested interests are composed of what we believe that we have to gain or lose by the outcome of a debate, discussion, decision, or event. These interests can be tangible (gaining or losing a job, money, or rank, for example) or intangible (gaining or losing respect, dignity, or self-esteem). Unacknowledged, they are, like assumptions, the enemies of intelligent discourse and constructive debate. It is only possible to have a valid and unbiased exploration of ideas if those with vested interests in the outcome either stand aside or openly acknowledge their situation so that others can consider their arguments in the light of that knowledge.

Among actions that help to keep vested interests from biasing the discussion are the following:

- Encourage "recusal"—a legal term in which judges or others with decision-making authority acknowledge their vested interest in a certain issue and voluntarily choose not to participate in the discussion.
- Use a facilitator for the discussion who is empowered to ask participants about possible vested interests, even during the "heat of the battle." It is generally better to have someone do this who is seen as neutral on the issue.
- Once a number of alternative ideas have been proposed, have a frank discussion about potential vested interests— what various groups or individuals may have to gain or lose under each scenario. This can be useful in removing any errors related to wishful thinking—for example, *"This would have the best outcome for this team, so it must be the best solution."*

If it appears that conflicting vested interests are at stake, the team should consider using other strategies, such as negotiation (to mention only one), to resolve differences that cannot be resolved through debate and logical problem-solving.

Shared Values

Members of a group or team can agree on their shared values and use them to develop rugged criteria by which to test their ideas. In particular, operational values, which encourage excellence and innovation, are key to the development of high-quality ideas. Operational values are those that are not just aspirations—how we would like to be—but also are translated into policies and practices and, above all, form the basis for making important decisions.

By definition, shared values cannot be imposed. They can be developed by and agreed to by the team, or they can be made so explicit that anyone joining that team or organization knows and accepts that he or she is buying into that set of values. Then they must be demonstrated and applied in a consistent way when making decisions and choosing actions.

Shared values regarding quality and innovation are especially useful in constructive debate when they are the basis of criteria for evaluating ideas. Ideally, participants should agree to these criteria early in the process—after a problem, issue, or opportunity has been framed but before participants have become so attached to a particular idea that they cannot be neutral in framing criteria. Decision criteria provide a relatively neutral way to evaluate ideas against one another or for their relevance to the issue. They should be applied during periods of "integration" where ideas are selected for further development.

Compelling Issues

Of course, a debate about something that nobody is very interested in is unlikely to produce useful results. A precondition to a lively discussion is that the problem or issue must be framed in a clear, compelling way. You can usually find many ways to frame a particular problem, each frame containing a set of possible ideas or solutions. At the same time, having a frame limits the thinking of participants, and thus ideas that fall outside that frame are unlikely to be raised, explored, or taken seriously even if they happen to be mentioned. For this reason, using multiple frames expands the potential universe of solutions.

Some actions that teams can take to make sure an issue or problem is worth discussing and debating include:

- Frame the problem in more than one way, and look for problem frames that are unusual or even provocative.
- Keep the problem statements brief; begin each statement with a phrase such as:
  - *"How can we . . ."*
  - *"What are some options to achieve . . ."*
- Focus on the future and what you want to achieve, rather than on the past and why the problem exists.
- Make sure everyone in the group is aware of the benefits of solving the problem or is responding both to the opportunity and to any consequences of a failure to act.

Clear and Effective Processes

Finally, an agreed-on process for constructive debate will ensure that most of the conditions above are met. You will find a number of tools and techniques to be useful in such a process, including:

- Invite or appoint a neutral facilitator.
- Establish the facilitator's role clearly at the beginning of the meeting.
- Have a clear agenda sent to participants in advance, allowing them time to think about the topic before the meeting.
- Establish, clarify, and agree on a set of norms for the discussion, and then enforce them. (See "Norm-Setting" in appendix 3.)
- Alternate between generating and building on ideas, and evaluating and selecting ones to move forward. (Two useful terms are "diffusion" and "integration." Diffusion means opening up to many different ideas and sugges-

tions, while integration means focusing on a few preferred ones. See "Diffusion/Integration Rule" in appendix 3.)

- Do not allow evaluation during the diffusion period, but do encourage it during the integration period. Consider appointing a temporary "devil's advocate" to critique ideas that seem to be moving forward without enough examination.

- Take an occasional "Reflection Break" to see how the process is working, whether people are getting enough "air time" for their ideas, and whether the norms are being followed. (See "Reflection Break" in appendix 3.)

- Record any potential decisions in an open way (on an actual or virtual whiteboard or flipchart, or by some other means that allows all to see what they are deciding about). Do this during the meeting and when you do this also ask for agreement or disagreement.

10 ■ Facilitating the Process of a Constructive Debate

A well-facilitated meeting can consist of an effectively executed agenda, full participation, active discussion, and meaningful outcomes. Although some organizations have available facilitation services, most groups need to operate on their own. This means that each participant needs to be aware of how to help facilitate a meeting. In general, it's better to have someone other than the formal leader performing that function, because it may be difficult for the leader or the participants to separate the two roles.

A constructive debate has a natural flow to it. It begins with framing the issue, then moves back and forth between Expressing Ideas and Engaging Others. The facilitator helps the group to focus on a few promising ideas, which are then explored in greater depth, tested, and challenged. At this point, further narrowing occurs, leading to a decision process. Figure 6 depicts this natural flow.

While no debate in the real world follows this pattern in a lockstep way, an effective facilitator will sense when the group needs to

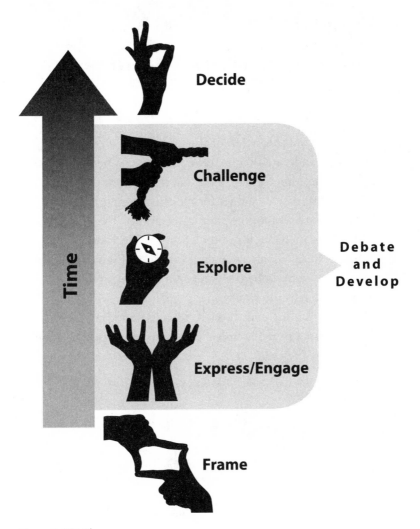

Figure 6: CD Flow

move forward or perhaps return to an earlier process, and will find ways to help it do so. For example, if a debate process seems to be stuck or circular, reframing the issue may stimulate new ideas.

If no professionally trained facilitator is available, the role can be shared (perhaps rotating among members for a meeting or even for a set period of time, and handed off temporarily when the person taking that role wants to be engaged in the content). Before initiating shared facilitation, though, make sure that the role is clear and, if possible, ask an experienced facilitator to conduct the first session so that less experienced members have a model to follow.

Framing the Issue

One of the first and most important tasks for the facilitator is to help the leader and participants frame the issue. When you frame a problem or issue, you are framing some things in and some things out. You are creating a container for meanings, implications, values, solutions, memories, emotions, and associations. The narrower the frame, the more predictable are the contents. The more predictable the contents, the less likely your solution can be innovative.

A good exercise to do before you begin working on an issue is to find several different ways to frame it. Each frame will invite a different kind of thinking and thus a different set of ideas. One useful way to frame issues or problems that demand action is to begin with the words "How can we . . . ?"

- *"How can we resolve the ongoing conflict between Engineering and Sales?"*
- *"How can we build greater collaboration between Sales and Engineering?"*
- *"How can we design a system that supports cross-functional alignment?"*

The way we frame a problem for debate can bias a group toward a particular solution or give an advantage to one side of an issue over another. For example, George Lakoff, Ph.D.,[10] of the University of California–Berkeley, has pointed out that framing issues related to taxation as "tax relief" creates an advantage for those who consider taxes too high. If you are providing "relief," there must be an affliction. Thus, it is difficult to be against "tax relief." However, framing the same issue as "investment in infrastructure" such as interstate highways and expanding Internet to more users produces a different reaction, because it is also difficult to appear to be against responsible future investment.

The way an issue is framed determines how people think and feel about it. The frame can thus create an opening to new and unusual ideas. Your frame should, of course, be factually based and non-judgmental. That means there is no implication in the statement about:

- Causes (who or what is to blame)
- Solutions (how the problem should be resolved)
- Political correctness in the organization (the answer the "powers that be" would like to hear)

To achieve a truly constructive exchange of ideas, as opposed to bickering from fixed positions, the participants in a constructive debate should agree on a frame for the issue at hand that is sufficiently broad, neutral, and interesting to provoke deep thought and creative energy rather than intense emotion or the fervor of conviction. (There is certainly a time for those emotions, once the ideas are developed and ready to be sold to other stakeholders!)

Reframing as an Intervention

Of course, sometimes discussions and debates reach a dead end. Ideas just stop flowing. Little enthusiasm is expressed for any solution— or a deadlock is reached among a limited set of ideas. As a facilitator, leader, or team member, you might then suggest reframing the issue so as to generate a different set of solutions. If you have already framed it in more than one way, you have some options available. If not, you can still ask: *"How else might we think about this problem or opportunity? What would be a different way to frame it?"*

Reframing is a technique for interpreting the available data surrounding a situation, result, or solution in an alternative way. To be effective, a reframe must:

- Take all relevant facts into account
- Provide a rational explanation or interpretation of those facts

- Align with the team's or another person's values, goals, and model of the world
- Be acceptable to you as an alternative way of viewing the idea or situation

When reframing, you will identify key goals, values, or elements of the target person's or the team's worldview. You will identify relevant facts concerning the situation or idea and will think of one or more alternate ways to interpret those facts that fit the criteria above. Ways to reframe a problem include:

- Try reversing cause and effect (when you can see that there is implied causation in the original frame): *"What if B caused A, rather than the other way around?"*
- See the problem through a different set of lenses: *"How might marketing look at it? Customers? Competitors?"*
- Select different aspects of the data set to emphasize: *"Let's consider the cultural implications of this change."*
- Identify the assumptions behind the original frame and ask, *"What if we didn't believe that? How might we then think about the problem?"*

If we believe that there is only one way to look at a problem, and thus a limited set of solutions, we may miss creative options—or even obvious ones that show up when we look at the problem from another point of view. Flexibility during the process of a debate—that is, being willing to temporarily set aside our preferred assumptions, beliefs, and frame—allows new ideas to emerge.

The Role of the Facilitator

The successful facilitator lives by an old Chinese proverb: "When the best leader's work is done, the people say, 'We did it ourselves.'" The essence of facilitation is to stay out of the limelight and focus on non-obvious ways of helping people to do the work they need to do. Some of the ways a successful facilitator does this are:

- Building and enforcing norms
- Managing the discussion process and handling questions

- Managing agenda and time
- Modeling good communication behaviors
- Making sure everyone has a chance to contribute and to be heard
- Suggesting and directing processes for achieving specific results
- Keeping the group focused on its real objectives
- Calling for, summarizing, and recording decisions
- Asking for and recording action steps and commitments

Dealing with Unconstructive Debate Behaviors

Some of what passes for "debate" in today's polarized media sounds rather more like a screaming match or a playground name-calling contest. Unfortunately, as more and more people are exposed to this style of (non)communication, some of it has filtered into corporate meeting rooms and teleconferences. As a leader, member, or facilitator, you may one day find yourself facing such a situation, so it's best to be prepared. Following are some guidelines to keep in mind.

- Keep your cool. Never allow a personal attack or accusation to push your defensiveness buttons, or you may find yourself the focus of a feeding frenzy.
  - o Example: *"What is the concern behind that question?"*
- Stay rational. Your adversary may prefer to fight the issue on an emotional or polarized basis. Your best offense is to remain perfectly reasonable.
  - o Example: *"That's an interesting point of view. . . . How did you arrive at that conclusion?"*
- Ask the other person to clarify their position or rationale. Do this calmly but persistently until you think you understand it (even though you may not agree).
  - o Example: *"What's the basis for your position? Please explain your rationale to me."*
- Recognize a "trap question" and rephrase it as that person's opinion rather than trying to answer it.

    ○ Example: *"I gather from your question that you disagree with me about . . ."*

- Don't allow yourself to be interrupted before finishing a thought; insist on your airtime.
    ○ Example: *"Hold on for a moment! I'd like to finish my thought, then I'd be interested in hearing your response."*

- When you paraphrase the other person's point, do it in a way that makes the statement sound more reasonable or intelligent than you actually think it is, rather than going down the tempting (but dangerous) path of making that person sound bad, wrong, or stupid.
    ○ Example: *"So, from your point of view, you would suggest . . . [X, Y, or Z]. Do I have that right?"*

- Don't allow an inaccurate characterization of your views to stand. Stop the process, if necessary, and correct the person publicly, but politely, by restating your opinion or idea.
    ○ Example: *"No, that is not an accurate reflection of my opinion. I said . . ."*

- Look for an opportunity to consider a point the other person is making, in a constructive and rational way, even if you still disagree with it.
    ○ Example: *"Before you continue, let me make sure I have understood your point. You think . . ."*

- Use a presumptive question to learn the strength of the other's opinion.
    ○ Example: *"Are you saying that there are NO circumstances under which you would consider . . . ?"*

- If the other person does not give you any airtime, interrupt when he or she pauses for breath, but only to paraphrase, in a non-evaluative way, a point the person has made (*not* to insert your thoughts). Pause for a split second, then say why you disagree.
    ○ Example: *"You've made an interesting point about . . . [pause]. Here's where I disagree . . ."*

Every participant in a constructive debate will find opportunities to use these tactics from time to time. Even the most collaborative teams will confront difficult issues where feelings run high, and when anger, fear, or the fierce defense of a position threaten to turn a productive conversation into something of a bar fight. The goal of these tactics is to avoid escalating occasional unconstructive behavior into interpersonal conflict, while keeping a focus on solving the problem or taking advantage of the opportunity.

Emotion is always present when human beings interact. It can take the form of enthusiasm, commitment, enjoyment, or other positive feelings that enhance the process. If emotions turn negative and start to disrupt the process, that may be time for a temporary disengagement. This can take the form of a quick caffeine break, a reschedule, a "time-out" to focus on the process, or even just a little bit of self-deprecating humor. (*Warning:* never use sarcasm—a form of humor that is inevitably experienced as negative feedback and virtually always escalates the already-difficult situation.)

11 ■ Developing and Maintaining a Culture and Processes that Encourage Breakthrough Solutions

Constructive debates don't just happen because people read a book or attend a class, though the will and the skill are both important and necessary. Rather, they should take place within the larger system of the organization. Organizations that wish to nurture and develop breakthrough solutions and bring them to market need to develop a culture and a set of processes that reshape the way the leaders go about exploring, developing, and deciding to move an idea forward to implementation. Organizational culture involves a complex set of systems; we can only touch on the topic briefly here. Culture is hard to see when you're inside it—the "what is water to a fish?" metaphor is relevant. Yet we can't ignore the role of organizational culture any more than fish can avoid the presence of water, for without it we can't actually exist. Given this combination of complexity and omnipresence, the work of changing an organization's culture is daunting—and many people give up before they even begin. But system change *can* begin with tweaks or "hacks": small changes that provide a "nudge" to leaders, managers, and others—a slight prod that makes it easier to follow the relevant guidelines and practices than to oppose them.

In their best-selling book, *Nudge: Improving Decisions About Health, Wealth, and Happiness,*[11] Professors Richard Thaler and Cass Sunstein define a "nudge" as a small feature of the environment that attracts attention and alters behavior. Two examples they describe are the fly painted near the drain in urinals in a men's room at Amsterdam's Schiphol Airport that reportedly reduced "spillage" by 80 percent, and the effect of having employees "opt-out" rather than "opt-in" to a retirement plan. Since not deciding takes considerably less energy than making decisions, these seemingly small changes can have large effects.

Nudges can be rewards or incentives for doing the "right thing," disincentives or inconvenience arising through not doing the right thing, defaults that make decisions easy or unnecessary, or competitions with others, even bets that maintain behaviors through the pain of losing an existing investment.

So, how can leaders make it easier for people to have a robust and constructive debate—the kind that can lead to real breakthroughs—rather than passing mediocre ideas along? What kind of nudge would it take for project leaders and managers to include and engage their teams first in generating better ideas, and then to give those ideas a thorough vetting by running them through a process that toughens and refines them?

Cultural Factors

Organizational cultures, like national or ethnic ones, consist of norms, values, taboos, rituals, and mythology, often among many other elements. Norms govern how people behave; values articulate what they believe in or strive for; taboos warn them about what is forbidden; rituals celebrate and reinforce what the organization finds important and valuable; and the mythology translates all these elements into stories that help people know what is expected and rewarded and how to be successful. All these factors can support a constructive debating process . . . or can seriously undermine it.

Norms: How We Behave

Explicit norms—that is, ones that are stated, discussed, included in orientations, or posted in actual or virtual meeting rooms—provide guidance as to behavior. Norms such as the following can, if made explicit and then enforced, create a generative climate:

- Defer evaluation of ideas until later in the process.
- Don't stop at the first good idea; generate many ideas.
- Build on the ideas of others.

Values: What We Believe In

Values form the basis of our most important decisions. They describe what we aspire to and are thus usually the foundation of both mission and vision. Here are some values that help create the conditions for vibrant and healthy debate:

- We celebrate our company's diversity of background and opinion.
- We encourage speaking truth to power.
- We support intelligent risk-taking.

Taboos: What Is Forbidden

Taboos can set off the organizational immune reaction. When articulated by leaders, taboos shape behavior even more strongly than norms. Unfortunately, many taboos are not explicit—and some may even reinforce caution and conflict avoidance when they are activated. Here are a few "positive" meeting taboos that can help in the idea-development process:

- Don't stop at the first decent idea.
- Don't step on ideas too early, but . . .
- Don't withhold your critique until it's too late.

Rituals: What We Celebrate

Rewards and public recognition are common rituals in organizations. In any culture, what is rewarded is generally repeated, so it's wise to reward and recognize what we want more of. Ideally, rituals should take place in addition to any celebrations of more-traditional success in the marketplace, since the focus here is on the early part of the process, before you know about results. Rituals that may help promote better ideas include:

- Giving an award to the team that came up with the most unusual or innovative prototype in a contest about new products or services
- Celebrating the failure we learned the most from this year
- Recognizing (with a lunch or small gift) the individual or team that contributed the highest number of different ideas to improve organizational processes

Mythology: Stories that Define the Culture

Even though norms and taboos may be implicit—that is, not stated directly—they can often be clearly communicated through stories. Many times, the way new employees learn how to fit in is through the stories others tell them about what has worked and what has not. For example, a story about a lab worker who used company equipment during off-hours to develop an innovation that became a valuable product suggests that asking for permission is not always required.

For each of these cultural factors, examples could be cited that could have a dampening or destructive impact on ideation and decision-making. An implicit norm that you don't criticize your manager; a value of requiring complete consensus on all decisions; a taboo against open conflict; rituals that only recognize success after a product is actually in the market; or stories about people who took a risk, failed, and were never heard from again—these are all predictors of fear, analysis paralysis, and stale ideas.

Processes, Practices, and Structures

The way things happen, the route that information travels, and the arrangements for getting work done all have a strong impact on ideation, development, and decision-making.

Two processes that could "nudge" (there's that word again) an organizational system or team toward better ideation and decision-making practices are based on research by psychologists.

Paul C. Nutt, in his 2002 book, *Why Decisions Fail*,[12] discusses his research on 78 major decisions by senior managers. He found that in only 15 percent of the cases was there a stage at which the managers sought alternative options. In a later study, he found that only 29 percent of managers consider more than one option; he also found a strong correlation between the number of alternatives considered and a decision's ultimate success. If managers or team leaders require themselves or their team members to ask for a greater number or variety of ideas before moving toward a decision, they will increase their chances of success.

Gary Klein, Ph.D., developed the practice of a "pre-mortem," in which project teams look into the future and imagine that their project has failed miserably. They then discuss what happened to make that result occur. This is a form of a behavioral skill (one we discussed in chapter 7) called "Anticipate Consequences." This behavior can lead to a deeper discussion on how to prevent these consequences or which alternative solution might be more successful.

These practices and similar ones that require conscious consideration of the downside of potential solutions, such as formal or informal scenario planning, can become standard meeting procedures. They can be included in boilerplate templates for planning meetings—saving leaders or facilitators the trouble of creating a plan from scratch or going into an important meeting with no plan at all. In other words, these are defaults that, if practiced repeatedly, can reshape meeting processes to make constructive debate more likely.

Additional helpful practices in meetings include:

- Assigning a "devil's advocate" to make and summarize arguments *against* a proposal. Because it is an assigned role, built into the meeting plan, the personal risk of critiquing is diminished.

- Having a standard practice of taking the last five minutes of a meeting to reflect on the process, using questions such as:
  - *What worked well in the way we generated [evaluated, or made decisions about] ideas?*
  - *What did we miss or avoid dealing with?*
  - *How satisfied are you with our process today? [Ask for a show of hands, with five fingers for "very satisfied" down to one finger for "very dissatisfied."] What should we do differently next time?*
- Stopping the process in the middle of a discussion, before making a decision, to ask participants how comfortable they feel right then with their own level of participation. Use a similar show of hands (five fingers down to one). Then ask what to change to make sure everyone has an opportunity to weigh in.

Many of the interventions discussed in the materials in the appendix can also be useful as part of a standard practice. In addition to interventions, you'll find tools that can make meetings more efficient, creative, collaborative, and interesting.

Not all constructive debates, of course, will take place in a formal meeting. In a 1:1 or small and informal meeting, it's a good practice to establish the agenda, norms, and processes by agreement before diving into the content. Step out of the content from time to time to listen and summarize and to ask if other people have some reflections or comments to offer. Check for agreement before moving to a decision. Put all agreements and commitments in writing, and later disseminate them, to make sure you understand them in the same way.

Rewards and Recognition

As we've probably all noticed from our own experience, what gets rewarded gets repeated. This is a neutral process—we develop both good and bad habits through experiencing rewards (sound diet choices leading to better health vs. addiction to drugs or alcohol because of the immediate hit of pleasure, for example). Short-term rewards are hard to resist. You may have seen the videos of children in some variant of the Marshmallow Test, struggling with the researcher's directive that they can have one marshmallow immediately, but two if they can postpone eating it for several minutes. The conclusions of this study about self-control leading to success later in life were recently cast into doubt as the researchers had failed to consider other important factors such as socioeconomic status. Nevertheless, the popularity of the videos suggests that we can identify with the emotional response to rewards. The shorter-term reward of immediate approval by a group or a leader can drive behavior, especially if no longer-term and more important reward is available, such as a positive performance review based on behaviors the organization wants to encourage.

Thoughtful design of rewards that support building better ideas rather than encouraging conflict avoidance or strict consensus (to give only two examples) can create "nudges" in the strategic direction the organization has chosen. An expectation, for instance, that managers include people from diverse backgrounds in *all* their project teams can become part of performance and reward discussions.

Leader Behavior

The role of a leader, whether formal or informal, is to set a standard to be emulated and a direction to be followed. Even when leaders in a hierarchical organization try to take a step back or suggest that they're "just going to be a member of the group," most people junior to them will not take them at their word. The leaders need to take conscious, repeated actions to minimize their impact in any meeting where they want ideas to flow without the filter of "political correctness."

As discussed earlier, meetings can be designed in ways that keep the leader from taking up too much room in the conversation. In addition, whether in a large meeting or a 1:1 conversation, leaders can support constructive debate by:

- Being clear at the beginning about anything that is off-limits or "taboo," so that others can feel free to range widely in their thinking without imagined restrictions
- Modeling constructive debate behaviors, especially the Engaging ones
- Providing positive feedback to team members about their use of the constructive debate behaviors, thereby reinforcing them
- Avoiding both positive *and* negative evaluation of the ideas themselves until later in the process (otherwise there will be a tendency to support the ideas the leader likes rather than exploring more widely—or to suppress ideas that seem less attractive to those who have more power)
- Withholding their opinion for some time during a decision-making process so they don't give clues as to "the right answer"
- When criticized, responding with curiosity rather than defensiveness

Organizations can move toward building better ideas by establishing cultural and process elements that encourage healthy competition as well as broad participation. They can set new standards of acceptable behavior and can reward a good process even before the results are in. They can design the organization to maximize participation and engagement by a diverse population. They can create small nudges in the right direction—norms, rituals, team and decision structures, meeting plans, expectations, rewards, and other ways that make it easier to be courageous, to be collaborative, and ultimately to achieve breakthrough solutions.

Conclusion

Building Better Ideas

As mentioned earlier, every day, ideas will walk out the actual or virtual door of your organization between the ears of employees, never to be taken advantage of by you. Some of them will be ordinary, some will be small but useful, some may be the seeds for breakthrough solutions. As long as they remain where they are—or move on to another organization—they are *not* helping you to achieve your tactical or strategic goals. And as long as your people keep their opinions to themselves about how to improve the ideas that do get a hearing, second-class suggestions will move forward. As a formal or informal leader or a business partner to those who are in such roles, you have an opportunity to change the status quo.

A Formula for Change

For many years in my consulting work, I've used a variant of David Gleicher's formula[13] to help people think about how to help change to happen. It looks like this:

$$(D \times V \times S) > R + C$$

D = *Dissatisfaction with the present state*
V = *Vision of the future*
S = *Support for making the change*
R = *Resistance to the change (related to risk and cost)*
C = *Change*

Gleicher's insight was that both people *and* organizations tend to change voluntarily when a certain combination of circumstances arises. But they must feel enough dissatisfaction with the status quo, have a positive vision of an alternative future state, and acknowledge a real belief that support will be available for helping them make the change effort. The combination must be strong enough to overcome the resistance to a particular change. If any of these three factors is absent, the product will be 0—and thus it's unlikely that people will choose to get on board with the change.

If you want to lead your organization toward a culture that supports constructive debate for the purpose of building robust ideas—ones that can become successful innovations for your company or organization—you can apply this insight. You can even (though this may seem counterintuitive) increase dissatisfaction with the status quo. You might decide to do this by providing disconfirming information, such as sales data showing reductions or an example of a competitor's growing market share or negative feedback from an important customer. You can share with or engage others in developing an alternative success vision. You can design support systems for the needed changes, such as training, coaching, or consulting assistance. You can also take actions that mitigate or reduce the costs and risks inherent in the change, thus reducing resistance.

Creating, supporting, and sustaining a culture that allows good ideas to become great ideas and mediocre ideas to be sidelined will take time and focused action. It will require attention to norms, values, taboos, rituals, and the organization's mythology. It will mean a rigorous review of systems, structures, and processes that may block or prevent open, inclusive, two-way communication about ideas. You will want to gain greater insight into the way we humans make decisions, by attending to the work of neuroscientists and behavioral economists. You will need to look at your own and others' leadership behavior and then try to extinguish the leadership "tics" that send unintentional messages, provoke apathy, go-along-to-get-along behavior, or even fear. And you will need to develop ever-greater skills in promoting open, vigorous, constructive debates. Here are a few principles to keep in mind.

Principles of Constructive Debate

- Develop and enforce norms that support discussion and open communication about controversial issues.
- More ideas lead to better ideas; avoid seeking the "one right answer."
- Balance creative and critical thinking; encourage a bias toward innovation.
- Check your title and your vested interests at the door—don't "wear" your ideas and opinions on your sleeve.
- Balance advocacy and inquiry—know where you are in the conversation, then make conscious choices.
- Stay open-minded—be willing to challenge your own assumptions as well as those of others.
- Ask for and guide feedback; then, without defending, justifying, or blaming, listen to it and say "thanks!"
- Replace defensiveness with curiosity.
- Focus group energy on the idea, not on the person who has offered it.
- Listen with curiosity and as an ally to any new idea; avoid being a knee-jerk critic or fan.
- Respond to challenges with Engaging and Exploring techniques (described in chapters 6 and 7).
- Move down the Ladder of Inference (see chapter 2) frequently and be alert to any actions or avoidance that could allow unexamined or unchallenged ideas to move toward decision and action.

This may sound onerous, but complex systems both resist and respond to change in any part of the system. The easiest person to change is *yourself,* so look for some small ways to begin where you have the most influence and be part of the larger effort through your example and advocacy.

Courage

Speaking up and speaking out both require courage—even more so if one's ideas are innovative, different from "common wisdom," or perhaps threatening to the status quo. Courage is more than a personal characteristic; it's also a response to the environment. The greater the trust we have in others around us and in the system, the more we are willing to take intelligent risks, believing that others will "have our backs." We all gain courage from feeling a sense of support from our colleagues, as well as having a set of norms and principles that support curiosity, questioning, and the challenging of assumptions. Freedom from fear and intimidation is basic to an environment that nurtures creativity, innovation, intelligent risk, and positive growth and change.

Collaboration

Organizations that encourage and reward internal, cross-boundary collaboration will reap the benefits of diversity and "beginner's mind." In this way, they enhance creative thinking and problem-solving, using a variety of the rich resources available across the organization. By bringing people together to engage in constructive debates, they establish a practice of enlisting people with differing backgrounds to assess and improve ideas that can ensure the organization's success. By declaring taboo the "not-invented-here" attitude, they enlarge possibilities for new ideas to get a hearing.

Breakthrough Solutions

Truly innovative solutions are the product of a rigorous process[14] of searching for important unmet needs and generating options; exploring, developing, selecting, and prototyping the most promising ideas; committing to the very best ideas and the resources required to fulfill them; realizing the product, service, process, or experience through high-quality project teamwork; and optimizing the ideas through reviewing, learning, improving, and applying them in new ways.

A process and an ethic of deep collaboration, fearless creativity, and honest critique are required throughout this "Innovation Journey" so that you can make true breakthroughs. Practices such as those we've discussed in this book can help achieve this; open, ethical, and nondefensive leadership practices are essential, as is a recognition that all of us in today's fast-paced and complex world need to continuously develop our skills in discussion, debate, providing feedback, and collaboration.

Debate can be constructive, disagreement can be collaborative, conflict can be creative.

Meanwhile, back in the break room . . .

"That was an amazing meeting!"

"I'm really excited about the possibilities we came up with!"

"I feel as if I'm part of a really high-performing team. You guys are so creative!"

"I can't wait to get started on the next challenge—we're on a roll!"

And not far away, in the hall near the manager's office . . .

"I wonder why I never knew what a great, innovative team they could be. It's as if we hired a completely different bunch of people—but they were here the whole time! I just didn't know how to tap into their minds. I didn't realize how much I was missing."

"Don't sell yourself short—it took some real courage to change your approach. That was a key part of the team's success. I hope you'll share your experiences with other leaders. I think the culture here might finally be ready to change."

Building and Enforcing Norms

Norms or ground rules are agreements about how members of the group will behave toward one another and how they will treat the ideas that are discussed. To be useful, norms must be clear, observable, agreed to, and enforced. Otherwise, they quickly lose their meaning and efficacy. Norms can be enforced in a matter-of-fact way (as when reminding yourself or others that someone has overstepped) or with humor (one group I worked with threw a paper airplane at anyone who broke a norm). Any enforcement tools used should be used consistently; they become a part of the culture of an ongoing group or team and shape behavior in observable and implicit ways.

The first time a group meets, they can establish and agree on a set of norms that will support constructive debate. These norms can be revisited before each session; attention to the norms can be evaluated at the end of the session, and they should be modified as necessary. Groups that meet regularly can record the norms they agree on and revisit them at each meeting to make sure they remain relevant and explicit.

Examples:
- Agree to confidentiality: "what is said here stays here."
- Ask questions and express disagreement openly.
- Ask for and offer constructive feedback.
- Silence electronics.

- Honor time limits.
- Listen as an ally.

Once norms have been established, and provided that they are enforced, they will generally prove useful throughout the life of a group or team. Others may be added as the need arises. The facilitator or members of the group can refer to them at strategic moments to redirect the conversation down more-helpful paths or to remind the group what they agreed to. For example, a facilitator might say, "Remember, we agreed not to evaluate until we had all the ideas on the table." From time to time, a facilitator or member might notice that an unhelpful, yet unspoken, norm exists (for example, "don't confront the boss"). They can call that to the group's attention and ask, "Do we want to keep that as a norm?"

Managing Discussions

In any organizational meetings, a great deal of learning takes place through dialogue and discussion. A good discussion isn't just a matter of luck—it needs to be managed. Questions are among the most valuable tools in a facilitator's kit for managing discussions. Statements can be another valuable tool but should be used sparingly so as to keep the discussion going. The ability to use both with clear intentions in mind has a powerful impact on both the quality and the amount of interaction in a meeting.

Questions or statements serve three main purposes in managing a discussion: They open the discussion, focus it, and close it. They guide the discussion to achieve specific objectives. When the objective has been achieved, it is time to move on.

Opening the Discussion
Purpose: To introduce the subject and engage the participants' thoughts and feelings.

- *"What ideas do you have about . . . ?"*
- *"How might we approach the issue of . . . ?"*
- *"What other ideas might we consider?"*

Focusing the Discussion

Purpose: To focus the participants' thoughts and ideas on specific ideas or solutions being considered.

- *"Tell me how you think that would work."*
- *"What would be the advantages of . . . ?"*
- *"What would be the disadvantages of . . . ?"*
- *"What are other examples of . . . ?"*
- *"Tell us more about . . ."*

Closing the Discussion

Purpose: To close the discussion and summarize key points or agreements, or to make a transition to the next topic. Statements are useful to close the discussion. Questions tend to open it up again.

- *"You made several key points here: . . ."* (summarize)
- *"Let's spend another 2 minutes on this topic and then move on."*
- *"Are we ready to move on to the next item?"*
- *"Can someone summarize where we are on this?"* (Or summarize a possible agreement as a "trial close.")
- *"So, you're agreeing to . . ."*

Handling Questions

Below is the sequence of behavior and thought that can guide you to the most appropriate choice of response for the specific situation.

- Acknowledge the questioner.
- Restate the question, ask for clarification.
- Decide if you should answer the question. If not:
  o Boomerang the question to the appropriate person or other meeting participants.
  o Facilitate the questioner's thinking about the question.
  o Defer the question to a later time; put it on the "Parking Lot"—see below for a description of this tool.

Using Interventions

If you are planning or leading a meeting, you will find certain tools and processes invaluable for moving it along productively. These tools can be called "interventions." An intervention is an activity designed to break into the status quo and create a shift. Interventions can be used to involve or engage participants, to help them maintain their focus, or to facilitate decisions and actions.

Involving or Engaging Participants

- *Write, then Speak*: Give participants a few minutes to jot down ideas on a specific topic, then use a process for sharing ideas such as the Round Robin (below) or any brainstorming process. This is useful when some participants tend to dominate the meetings and you are not hearing from some of the more thoughtful members, who may prefer time to reflect rather than "thinking out loud."
- *Round Robin*: Ask each participant to give her or his idea briefly or to pass. Then, go around the group one or more times. This ensures that everyone who has a contribution to make has an opportunity to make it. This is a classic form of brainstorming that is especially effective in meetings where different personalities or levels may make it difficult for some people to get their ideas out on the table.
- *Grouping and Regrouping*: Ask the group to form pairs, trios, or quads and come up with ideas or recommendations on a particular topic. They then report it out to the larger group. This is particularly useful when there are members who have trouble being heard or speaking up in a larger group.

Maintaining Focus

- *Parking Lot:* When an issue arises that is not relevant to the agenda item currently being discussed, write it on a flipchart page or whiteboard area labeled "Parking Lot." If the issue is relevant to a later item, raise it at the appropriate time in the meeting. If it is not relevant then, ask at the end of the meeting if, how, and when the group wants to handle the issue. By doing this, you keep the group on focus without appearing to ignore contributions and you make sure that issues with importance, but not imme-diacy, don't get lost.

- *Time Out:* When you think the group has strayed from its purpose, call a "Time Out" and ask whether the discus-sion is helping them get to where they want to go. (It may be helpful to remind them of the purpose and objectives of the meeting.) If they say a certain discussion is relevant, then step back and allow it to continue. If they say it is off purpose, then ask them what they would like to do instead.

- *Time Check*: When an issue is being discussed past the time allotted for it on the agenda, refer to the time already spent on the item, and ask whether the group wants to continue to discuss it, or set it aside for the time being (in which case you would put it on the Parking Lot for later action), or make a decision now, and so forth. If they want to continue discussing it, the group needs to agree on how they want to allot the remaining time for the meeting or whether they are willing to extend it.

Facilitating Decisions and Actions

Once the process of constructive debate has taken place, the group may continue by moving toward a decision. This may be because of time pressure (they have agreed to decide by the end of the meeting and that time is rapidly approaching), or because the issue has been thoroughly discussed and debated, or all partici-pants have had an opportunity to state their views and are ready to move forward. The facilitator can ask the group what they are ready to do.

Methods of Decision-Making:

- *Delegation* to an individual or subgroup to decide, with or without a group recommendation

- *Voting*
  - Majority (51 percent)
  - Supermajority (75 percent or other)
  - Ranking (Each person ranks his or her top choices, points are awarded—3 for #1, 2 for #2, and so on—and then points are tallied and the decision goes to the option with the most points.)
- *Point distribution* (Each person has a number of points to distribute; he or she may give them all to one option or distribute them among preferred options.)
- *Consensus* (Each person has an opportunity to express an opinion about a proposed option. If all agree, the decision is made. If a member of the group does not agree, he or she is asked to state his or her concerns or upgrades. The group makes a good-faith effort to deal with the concerns or suggestions and to modify the proposal to make it acceptable if possible. All members agree that the proposal should be implemented and agree either to accept and participate or to "disagree and commit," where one or more members disagree, but are still willing to commit to implementation.)

Unless the group has a common practice for decision-making, they will need to agree on how to make decisions on the topics under discussion. In some cases, different issues may have different decision methods. For example, something that everyone in the group will have to carry out may require a consensus. Decisions that fewer people will carry out or that are less important to the vested interests of members may simply require a majority vote recommendation or delegation of the decision to the person or people most involved.

When time pressure forces a decision, you can:

- Do a time check and remind the group that they committed to make the decision by the end of the meeting.
- Ask what it would take for them to be ready to decide. When they respond, make it happen if you can. (For example, they may say, "We haven't heard from [mem-

ber's name] yet." You can then ask that person what they think.)

- Conduct the agreed-on decision process.

When the group is ready to make a decision, if you or a group member perceive that an issue has been thoroughly discussed and that all points of view have been expressed (this sometimes becomes obvious when the discussion has become repetitive), you can:

- Check to make sure that all points of view have been expressed (you may use a Round Robin format, asking participants to add anything left unsaid or pass).
- Ask if the group is ready to make the decision. If so,
- Conduct the decision process.

Principles of Effective Facilitation

The principles below are relevant for any successful facilitation, but they are especially important for facilitating a constructive debate, where enthusiasm, emotional intensity, and hearty disagreement are to be expected and even encouraged. Good facilitation practices, such as these, can guide this energy into productive channels:

- Know the purpose of the meeting or conversation you are facilitating.
- Make sure the agenda is explicit and aligned with the purpose.
- Learn which items are for information, which are for discussion, and which ones require a decision.
- Gain agreement about the role you will take, early in the meeting.
- Maintain a neutral role regarding the content; if you can't, ask someone else to facilitate.
- Establish or review norms at the beginning of the meeting or conversation; make sure they are enforced.
- Agree on the process or processes to be used for decision-making, information-sharing, and any other key components of the meeting.

- Be aware of the difference between the content of the meeting and the process; as facilitator, your focus is the process.
- Be willing to call for a process check when you sense that the group has bogged down.
- Observe behavior and note patterns of participation, agreement or disagreement, and leadership.
- Provide feedback and suggest activities to the group, based on your observations, that will move the members toward the outcomes they hope to achieve.
- Make sure that everyone in the group has an opportunity to express ideas and opinions.
- Encourage the group to take action rather than avoid dealing with problems, issues, and decisions.
- If you sense that the group is avoiding dealing with an important issue or decision, remind the group of its purpose and ask if the current activity is helping them to achieve it.
- At the end of the meeting, summarize decisions and action items. Make sure they are recorded (graphically) and saved in a form that can be shared. Taking a photo of the flipchart or whiteboard and sending it around to meeting participants, or copying and sending the virtual whiteboard list of action steps, ensures that agreements and decisions are not lost or misremembered.

Appendix 2 ■ Constructive Debate Planning

Many of the forms shown throughout this section can be downloaded from https://www.barnesconti.com/CD/.

1. Frame the problem or issue in a way that is objective and neutral as to cause or solution.

   • Framed Issue:

   • Desired Outcome:

2. Identify key participants and note any possible vested interests in the outcome. Include yourself.

Participant	Opinion/Vested Interests

Place an asterisk (*) next to the name of anyone who could take a facilitator role or consider the use of a neutral facilitator under Step 4.

3. Review conditions for a constructive debate.
   - To what degree does each condition already exist? Mark that place on the scale and, below each, note 2 to 3 actions you could take to improve or reinforce those conditions.

Ability to communicate

| 1 | 2 | 3 | 4 | 5 | 6 | 7 |

Very little   To a great degree

Open-mindedness

| 1 | 2 | 3 | 4 | 5 | 6 | 7 |

Very little   To a great degree

Minimum of conflicting vested interests

| 1 | 2 | 3 | 4 | 5 | 6 | 7 |

Very little   To a great degree

Shared values

| 1 | 2 | 3 | 4 | 5 | 6 | 7 |

Very little   To a great degree

Compelling issues

| 1 | 2 | 3 | 4 | 5 | 6 | 7 |

Very little   To a great degree

Clear and effective process

| 1 | 2 | 3 | 4 | 5 | 6 | 7 |

Very little   To a great degree

4. Select and review 3 to 4 tools, approaches, or activities that may be useful during the discussion debate.
5. Develop a tentative agenda that includes the use of process tools as appropriate.

Activity	Process	Person	Time

6. Use the Observer Guide during or after the meeting to help the team members continue to develop and improve their skills.

Observer Guide

Skills		Name	Name	Name
EXPRESS IDEAS	Make suggestions			
	Offer reasons			
	Provide examples			
ENGAGE OTHERS	Ask for ideas			
	Ask for feedback			
	Listen actively			
EXPLORE VIEWS	Draw out			
	Build on ideas			
	Anticipate consequences			
CHALLENGE POSITIONS	Identify assumptions			
	Clarify rationales			
	Argue a point			

Many of the forms shown throughout this section can be downloaded from https://www.barnesconti.com/CD/.

Affinity Diagram

An affinity diagram helps you to categorize or identify relationships among ideas, issues, or elements of a system.

Materials/Equipment:
- Postable notes

Process:
1. Conduct a "silent brainstorming" session, preferably using postable notes.
2. Ask the group to rearrange the notes, posted on a wall or table, into categories of similar ideas.
3. Ask the group to create titles that label the sets of ideas. Use brief titles or headings that describe the theme of each category.

Applications:
- When you need to break a complex issue into broad categories
- When you need to organize ideas, solutions, or recommendations
- As a follow-up to a brainstorming process using postable notes

Brainstorming or "Note-Storming"

1. After formulating a problem statement or question, remind the group of the rules for brainstorming. They are:
   - Allow enough time for the activity to get beyond the tried and true ideas.
   - Emphasize quantity, not the quality of ideas.
   - Do not criticize, evaluate, or judge ideas, either for yourself or others.
   - Post ideas where all can see them.
   - Do not interrupt the process.
   - Encourage humor, "wild" or unique ideas, and a playful attitude.
   - Suspend hierarchical power.
   - Don't quit too soon.

Applications:
- When you want to generate a large number of ideas
- When you want to stimulate new ideas
- When you want to minimize "private ownership" of ideas and maximize cross-fertilization

2. Use either a Round Robin format (where each person contributes in turn) or a "Popcorn" style (where members contribute ideas as they occur).
   - Record all ideas on flipcharts or whiteboard.
   - Allow at least two 2-minute silences before stopping.
   - Alternative: have the group write their ideas on postable notes and place them on large sheets of paper or a board, reading other people's ideas as they do.

Consensus-Building

A consensus process results in a decision that will be implemented and supported by all members of the team even if they do not fully agree with it.

It is most useful when there is a history of discussion or previous understandings about the issue and where there is now a need for agreement or alignment.

Materials/Equipment:
- Note paper
- Flipcharts or whiteboard
- Markers

Applications:
- When you want to develop a new agreement
- When you need to work through mild to moderate disagreement about a decision
- When you need to make decisions about purpose, vision, values, policies, or practices that need the support of the entire team

Note: Use this tool after a discussion in which the issues are aired.

Version One

1. Clearly identify and state the issue under discussion; for example, "How would you describe the purpose of this team?"
2. Each person on the team writes down her or his response.
3. The facilitator asks for each person's response and writes it on a flipchart or whiteboard.
4. If there seems to be significant agreement, team members can try writing a statement that summarizes what each has said. If there are differences, go to the next step.
5. The facilitator asks the group to identify and highlight words or phrases they like in each statement, even if they do not agree with the whole statement.
6. Team members individually write a new statement, using as many as possible of the highlighted words or phrases. These are posted over the other ones and discussed. The group combines, modifies, and chooses a final statement with which they can all substantially agree. It may be necessary to repeat steps 5 and 6 another time to come closer to agreement.

7. If consensus is not entirely achieved, members who disagree are asked for the minimum change it would take to shape the statement to something they could support even if they don't fully agree. If the rest of the team agrees, these changes are made. If not, another tool for resolving conflict or building agreement should be used.

Version Two

This version of consensus-building is useful when you are developing new agreements that you want the entire team committed to implement or align with. Use an actual or virtual whiteboard or large paper roll (36 in. or 48 in.) and white movable tape (both can be purchased at art supply stores).

1. Clearly identify and state the issue under discussion; for example, *"What is the purpose of this team?"* The facilitator begins by asking, *"What word or phrase would you use to describe the purpose of this team?"*
2. Team members record the words or phrases on 8½ × 11 in. paper, writing with markers in large block letters so they can be read easily. They can record more than one word or phrase.

    If you are using a whiteboard or large sheet of white paper as a background, use colored paper for the words and phrases.
3. Individuals, in turn, write on or tape their responses to the whiteboard or paper, reading them aloud as they do so. Others may ask questions for clarification.
4. The facilitator, with direction from the team, moves similar words and phrases into groupings on the board or paper.
5. The team reviews groupings and identifies themes. They may want to move phrases or words around.
6. The facilitator asks the team to identify the words or phrases that best represent the purpose (or other issue under discussion).

7. The group combines, modifies, and chooses a final statement using the words and phrases the group has selected. They may do this in open discussion or (especially if there are many introverts in the group) by writing their own versions, then posting them and having the group choose or modify the one that best states what people are agreeing to.

8. If consensus is not entirely achieved, members who disagree are asked for the minimum change it would take to shape the statement to something they could support even if they don't fully agree. If the rest of the team agrees, these changes are made. If not, another tool for resolving conflict or building agreement should be used.

Cost/Benefit Analysis

Determining whether a solution is cost-effective is an important part of decision-making. Particularly when considerable resource increases are proposed, you will need to be able to show return on investment. This tool is also helpful in making decisions about whether to explore high-risk/high-reward options.

> **Applications:**
> - When you are choosing among alternative solutions
> - When action steps are likely to involve risk

Materials/Equipment:
- Prioritized action ideas
- Cost/benefit forms

Process:
1. Identify the costs or risks involved in the solution you have selected. Are there any hidden costs?
2. Identify or calculate potential benefits.
3. Compare potential costs and benefits. Is it worth the effort to achieve this?
4. Consider which risks could be adjusted to decrease the probability or consequences of failure.
5. Identify other ways to improve the cost/benefit ratio and recalculate.
6. Discuss, then check "Go," "Caution," or "No Go" as appropriate for each action idea.

In summary, the results of a good cost/benefit analysis can be represented as follows:

High

Potential
Costs

Low

| | Forget it | Explore it |
| Enhance it | Do it |

Low   High

**Potential
Benefits**

Application: Cost / Benefit Analysis

Idea	Potential Costs	Potential Benefits	How to Reduce Risk and Improve Cost/Benefit Ratio

1.

Go	Caution	No Go

2.

Go	Caution	No Go

3.

Go	Caution	No Go

Creative Controversy

One technique that can be used to derive both individual and organizational benefit from the conflict of ideas is called creative controversy.

Conflict, handled in this way, can become a stimulus for deeper and broader thinking on issues, using the content from entrenched positions either as the basis for a new synthesis or to generate innovative ideas. Instead of avoiding conflict, the parties embrace it through a series of structured activities. This may be done within the context of a team meeting or with the help of a facilitator.

Applications:
- When members have developed fixed positions and no movement is occurring
- When you want to explore a controversial issue
- When it is especially important for members to understand one another's opinions or ideas

The creative controversy process is basically as follows:

1. Clarify the issue with an agreed-on problem statement, and then develop clear position statements.
2. Each party to the conflict develops and presents the most compelling arguments in support of that position.
3. Each party listens to and clarifies the other's position until they believe that they understand it fully.
4. The parties then switch sides and argue as forcefully as possible for the other position.
5. The parties work to agree on a new, synthesized position or develop a new alternative that they can both support.

This process is an efficient way first to capture the energy tied up in strongly held positions and then to use it for resolution and innovation. New ideas frequently emerge from controversy.

Select a partner to work with on the exercise, then select one of the following controversial issues (or create your own). Choose the side that is closest to your own opinions or that you can agree to argue in favor of. Find another team that holds or will take the opposite position to yours on the issue.

You will have 10 minutes to select your strongest arguments, write them down, and put together a case for your position. Choose which team will present their arguments first. Each team will then be given 5 minutes to present their arguments. It will be helpful to take notes of the opposition's case. Ask questions to learn as much as possible about the other's point of view.

After each side has presented their arguments, switch sides and argue as forcefully as possible for the opposite point of view. Each team will be given 5 additional minutes to argue the opposite position. Both teams will then attempt to agree on a broader, more-informed position that synthesizes the arguments from both positions.

Medical Research

A. Decisions concerning medical research should be made primarily based on the potential social and economic benefits to the larger society.

B. Decisions concerning medical research should be made primarily based on the basis of commonly held values, morals, and beliefs of the members of a society.

Stimulating the Economy

A. The best way to stimulate an economy that is in recession is by providing corporations with incentives to spend money.

B. The best way to stimulate an economy that is in recession is by providing individuals with incentives to spend money.

Organizational Focus

A. This organization would be more successful if it focused more on what it does best and quit dabbling in what it doesn't know.

B. This organization would be more successful if it were to diversify more, so it could insulate itself from potential problems in one market sector.

Questions

- What, if any, change took place in your own opinion or position during the exercise?
- What helped move you to modify your position?
- How can you apply this experience to real controversies at work?

Diffusion/Integration Rule

This ground rule helps you keep the right balance between idea generation and decision-making. It should be discussed and agreed to early in a meeting or institutionalized as a team "norm" so it can be invoked at the appropriate time.

Process:

1. Divide the meeting or the topic into diffusion and integration periods.

2. During the diffusion period, generate as many different ideas as possible. No evaluation of these ideas is allowed. Members are encouraged to build on one another's ideas. The rules of brainstorming apply.

3. During the integration period, develop criteria for selection. Then test the ideas against the criteria, evaluate, prioritize, or choose. New ideas are not encouraged during this period, though it is important to leave a flipchart sheet up where people can write new ideas for the next diffusion session. Alternate as needed, while moving ahead toward a decision. For example, the first diffusion session may generate ideas for areas to focus on, then the integration session results in selecting one. The next diffusion period may generate specific project ideas within the area, so during the integration period the team selects three projects. The third diffusion period generates sources for funding, and so forth.

Applications:
- When there is a tendency to judge ideas too quickly
- When time pressure threatens to discourage creativity
- When your team is having trouble coming to closure and moving ahead with decisions
- When you need to balance efficiency and creativity

This can be done very effectively via electronic media over a period of time, posting ideas where they can be read by all.* Strict time limits will have to be enforced, however, in order to keep the

---

* This can be in the form of an interactive "blog" or a discussion forum.

process moving. (For example, all members receive the message "Post all of your ideas about possible quick-start applications by Friday.") It may be most effective to conduct the diffusion portion asynchronously to allow plenty of time for members to consider many possibilities and conduct the integration meetings synchronously.

Force Field Analysis

This tool helps you to identify the dynamics in a complex system that must be considered in resolving a problem or initiating a change.

Materials/Equipment:
- Flipchart or whiteboard
- Postable notes (optional)
- Markers

Applications:
- When you are confronted with a persistent problem
- When you want to analyze the dynamics affecting a problem or issue

Process:
1. Identify the process, situation, or issue to be analyzed.
2. List forces that are moving the issue toward improvement or resolution as well as the forces keeping the issue in place or moving against resolution. Use a form similar to the one illustrated below. Participants can use postable notes that are then transferred to the form; otherwise, a facilitator can conduct an open session.

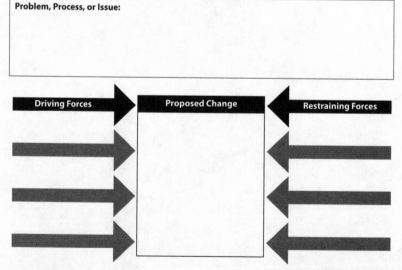

Problem, Process, or Issue:

Driving Forces   Proposed Change   Restraining Forces

3. When ideas have been collected, identify positive forces that can be enhanced and negative forces that can be reduced or eliminated.

Framing and Reframing

A frame of reference is the general background or context within which we consider an idea. The frame we use often determines how we feel and react. The way we frame a *problem* generally predicts the set of solutions we will consider. The way we frame a *debate* suggests the positions that participants will take. Reframing is a technique for interpreting the available data surrounding a situation, result, or solution in an alternative way. To be effective, a reframe must:

Applications:
- When the group seems "stuck" in discussing a problem or issue
- When creative thinking is required
- When you want the group to consider alternative points of view, approaches, or solutions

- Take all relevant facts into account to provide a rational explanation or interpretation of those facts
- Align with the target person's values, goals, and even model of the world
- Be acceptable to you as an alternative way of viewing the idea or situation. When reframing:
  o Identify key goals, values, or elements of the target person's worldview
  o Identify relevant facts concerning the situation or idea
  o Think of an alternate way to interpret those facts that fits the criteria above

Example:
- Your frame around the situation:
  —*"We should not use the vendor we have used before; they are not capable of the level of quality we require."*

Your Reframe:
  —*"Choosing this new vendor provides us with an opportunity to save some money and experiment with a new approach."*

From/To Analysis

This tool helps you to clarify goals as you begin to plan a strategy.

Materials/Equipment:
- Flipchart or whiteboard
- Markers
- Postable notes

Process:
1. On a flipchart, a long sheet of paper, or a whiteboard, draw a vertical bisecting line. Label the left side "From" and the right side "To."

Applications:
- When you are leading a change process
- As a follow-up to a visioning session
- When you are preparing to design a strategic solution to a difficult problem
- When you need concrete and specific change goals
- When you are designing metrics to measure change

2. Ask the group to review their vision statement and then identify specifically where they are now and where they will need to be in order to achieve the vision. You may want to define specific areas, such as "Financial," "Capabilities," and the like. The group can use postable notes, or a leader can facilitate and record. As an alternative, use graphic symbols rather than words to promote a deeper discussion.
3. As an alternative, ask the question more generally, and use an affinity diagram process to cluster the suggestions into categories.

Is/Is Not Matrix

The Is/Is Not Matrix is a tool for organizing data in ways that expose underlying patterns. Discovering such patterns helps localize a problem, making it easier to identify the cause of the problem. This analysis both precedes data collection (so the team or person will know what kind of differences to look for) and follows it (so the team can discover which factors actually affected the results).

Applications:

- When you have a specific problem to solve
- When a group can provide a "bigger picture" of where and how a problem occurs
- When you have specific bits of data on a problem and need to identify patterns

You can use an Is/Is Not Matrix to help pinpoint a problem by exposing where it does and does not occur. Such analysis lets teams avoid wasteful effort, directing their energies to the most potentially fruitful areas.

Materials/Equipment:

- "Is/Is Not Matrix—Example" or a simplified version on a flipchart or whiteboard.

Process:

1. Identify the problem or situation you want to analyze. Your process map may have identified a problem to analyze.
2. Use the Is/Is Not Matrix to organize your knowledge and information. This matrix can be re-created and used in virtually any setting. An individual may complete the matrix, or it can be used in a team.
3. Complete as many of the matrix cells as possible. The matrix cells can be filled in any order or sequence.
4. Look for relationships in the data presented. Some relationships or potential causes may be apparent once all information is entered into the cells. In certain instances, other problem-solving techniques or activities will need to be undertaken to further isolate causes and effects.

Is/Is Not Matrix—Example

Problem	Is Where, when, to what extent, or regarding whom does this situation occur?	Is Not Where, etc., does this situation NOT occur, though it reasonably might have occurred?	Therefore What might explain the pattern of occurrence and non-occurrence?
Where The physical or geographical location of the event or situation. Where it occurs or where it is noticed.			
When The hour, time of day, day of week, month, or time of year of the event or situation. Its relationship (before, during, after) to other events.			
What Kind or How Much The type or category of event or situation. The extent, degree, dimensions, or duration of the occurrence.			
Who (Do *not* use these questions to blame.) What relationship do various individuals or groups have to the situation or event? To whom, by whom, near whom, etc., does this occur?			

Norm-Setting

Version One

For new teams or mixed groups:

1. Ask the group what ground rules they would like to have that will help them to achieve the results they hope for.
2. Brainstorm a list of possible ground rules or norms.
3. Ask for clarification so you can make the behaviors observable.
4. Ask for agreement. If someone does not agree, ask what it would take for him or her to "sign up," then modify if possible and ask for agreement.
5. Ask how the group wishes to enforce the norms.
6. Rewrite and post the norms in a visible place.

> **Applications:**
> - When you want to establish a productive climate for discussion and debate
> - When discussion and debate become unproductive and you want to make some agreements that will improve quality and productivity

Version Two

For existing teams:

1. Ask the group to list current norms for team meetings.
2. Identify which are explicitly stated and which are implicit but real.
3. Ask if, and how, they would need to be modified to enable the group to meet expectations and avoid negative outcomes.
4. Ask how the group will enforce them.

On the Worksheet for Team or Meeting Norms, several areas are named in which groups or teams may want to suggest norms for meetings that will promote constructive debates.

Worksheet for Team or Meeting Norms

Category	
Communication	
Information-sharing	
Agenda and times	
Decision-making	
Problem-solving/Conflict management	
Focus vs. distractions	
Action planning	
Other	

Parking Lot

1. Place a flipchart page labeled "Parking Lot" where it can be seen by all team members (in person or by video conference).
2. When issues arise that are peripheral to the main topics of discussion, put them on the Parking Lot page.
3. At the end of the meeting, refer to the page and identify action steps for each item. *Caution:* If you don't follow up with this step, this tool will be seen as an "idea-killer" tool.

Applications:

- When you want to make sure the group remains focused on the issue at hand
- When you don't want to lose track of an important idea or issue that is not relevant to the current discussion
- When you want to demonstrate respect for a person who makes an off-topic but important comment

Plus/Delta Review

At the end of the meeting, take a few minutes to evaluate the session. Ask the group to think about what worked especially well (Plus) and what they would like to change for the next time (Delta). List all comments and make a point of reminding the group of what they want to keep or change at the beginning of the next meeting.

Applications:
- To call the group's attention to process
- To learn what worked well and what needs to be changed about a meeting process
- To check in with the group as to how it is progressing

+	Δ

Prioritizing

This is a method for getting a quick sense of a group's opinions or preferences.

Materials/Equipment:
- Flipchart or whiteboard and markers
- Colored "dots"

Applications:
- When several issues or solutions are under consideration
- As an early step in the decision-making process
- To narrow the field of choices

Process:
1. Clearly identify and state the issue under discussion; for example, *"What are the two most important goals for the team this year?"*
2. The team brainstorms a list from which to choose. The facilitator or recorder posts the list where all can see it.
3. Give each team member six (or another appropriate number*) colored "dots" that can be applied to the flipchart paper (these are available at stationery stores). Giving each person a number of check marks that he or she can use is also effective and does not require any additional supplies.
4. Team members then apply as many dots (or check marks) as they like to the items. They can apply all six dots to one item or can distribute them among several items.
5. The facilitator identifies the items receiving the most dots. The target number of items is considered selected. If a tie results, members can move their dots from nonselected items to the items still in competition.

---

* In general, the number of dots should be two or three times the number of items in the final outcome; that is, if the goal is to identify the two most important items, four or six dots would be appropriate. This method balances the amount of support for each item with the level of interest and commitment by individual team members. If only considering the level of support, give each member fewer dots; the rule is that each dot must be applied to a different item.

6. In virtual, synchronous meetings (such as video or computer conferences), ask members where they wish to place their "dots"—the facilitator then places them accordingly.

Reflection Break

Version One

For planned reflection breaks, questions can be prepared and written on flipcharts or the whiteboard. A good format for developing questions is:

- *"What?" "So what?" "Now what?"*
- *"What happened?" "What did you notice?"*
- *"So, what does it mean?" "What have we learned?"*
- *"Now, what shall we do about it?" "How can we apply what we learned?"*

Typical questions might include:

Applications:

- When you want the group to reflect on and upgrade the process they are using to achieve a particular result
- When the group process breaks down
- When something important occurs and you want the group to learn from the experience
- At the end of a session as a way of capturing and summarizing what has been learned and how to apply it

- *"What did we learn from that experience/discussion?"*
- *"What worked well in the meeting today?"*
- *"What could we do differently the next time?"*
- *"How can we improve . . . ?"*
- *"How were we able to accomplish . . . ?"*

1. Any of these or other questions can be asked as needed in the group—the member who is facilitating or another member can call for a reflection break. The purpose may be to "capture" learnings that might otherwise be forgotten or overlooked, to explore what has been going on in order to improve the process, or other purposes.
2. A time limit of 5 or 10 minutes is usually appropriate and should be stated up front.
3. The facilitator should make sure that everyone who has something to say is heard. If the team has one or two more extroverted members who tend to use more "air time," have people take 2 minutes first to think and jot down their reflections. Then get people's comments one at a time while

you record them on flipchart paper. This slows the process down enough to allow most people to participate fully.

4. At the end of the time allotted, the facilitator can summarize or ask for a summary, then ask the team what they want to do with the information (get it copied and pass it around, give it to a person or subgroup to follow up on, or other).

Version Two

1. For a quick "learning intervention," the facilitator can ask the team to step back from the task for 5 minutes and rate the process by holding up the appropriate number of fingers (1 = low, 5 = high). Use the following questions or others as appropriate.

   "To what extent are you satisfied with the way the team is working?"

   "To what extent are you satisfied with your own level of participation?"

2. Allow the team a few minutes to clarify responses and adjust the process, then return to the task.

Round Robin

Applications:

- When you want to poll the group by providing everyone in the group with an opportunity to contribute
- When some members are dominating the discussion and others are not participating at all

1. Present the question or issue to be discussed in the meeting.
2. Call for a Round Robin. That means that each person gives her or his idea or opinion in turn before any of the ideas are discussed.
3. Give the group a few minutes to think about or jot down ideas. Ask someone to start by giving one idea or offering a suggestion or opinion. The person to her or his left is next; move clockwise around the group. It is acceptable to pass.
4. The facilitator may record the ideas and may (or may not) participate in turn. (This format allows the facilitator to participate in idea-sharing; it is better *not* to participate if the task is to give opinions or make judgments.)
5. The activity may continue for several rounds until everyone passes or for a specific number of times.
6. No comments on ideas or opinions are permitted until the Round Robin is over. Then clarifications and a general discussion can follow.

Summarizing

The leader or facilitator invokes a "rule of summarizing." This means that new information cannot be added until the previous information has been reviewed and summed up to the satisfaction of the group or the other person. To be acceptable, a summary should be:

Applications:
- When members are not listening to one another and debates are becoming unproductive
- When members are wandering off topic

- Stated neutrally (*"Your point of view is . . ."* versus *"You stubbornly maintain that . . ."*); for example, shows neither agreement nor disagreement; does not judge
- Stated briefly
- Stated in one's own words rather than "parroted," thus showing an intellectual understanding of what the other has said
- Checked out with the originator of the statement; for example, *"You think we should go ahead with the project over Engineering's objections. Is that right, Susan?"*
- Before proceeding with their statement, the next speaker summarizes *either* what the relevant points of the discussion were (if the tool is being used to move toward a decision) *or* the previous speaker's statement (if the tool is being used to move toward resolution of a conflict).
- The leader or facilitator ensures that the summary has been accepted by the previous speaker(s) as substantially correct; that is, it shows understanding (not agreement) before the speaker continues.

Notes

1. Paul M. Romer, "Endogenous Technological Change," *Journal of Political Economy* 98, no. 5 (1990): S71–102.

2. Rogers Commission report (1986), "Report of the Presidential Commission on the Space Shuttle Challenger Accident."

3. Christopher Chabris and Daniel Simon, *The Invisible Gorilla: And Other Ways Our Intuitions Deceive Us* (New York, NY: Broadway Books, 2011).

4. "The Ladder of Inference" was first put forward by Argyris in 1990 and used in Peter Senge, *The Fifth Discipline: The Art and Practice of the Learning Organization* (New York, NY: Doubleday; rev. and updated ed., March 2006).

5. Elizabeth Morrison and Kelly See, "An Approach-Inhibition Model of Employee Silence: The Joint Effects of Personal Sense of Power and Target Openness," *Personnel Psychology,* 68, no. 3 (August 2015): 547–580.

6. I. L. Janis, *Groupthink: Psychological Studies of Policy Decisions and Fiascoes* (Boston, MA: Houghton Mifflin, 1982).

7. Erik Larsen, "New Research: Diversity + Inclusion = Better Decision-making at Work," *Forbes Magazine,* September 21, 2017.

8. Senge, *The Fifth Discipline.*

9. Scenario planning involves identifying several stories about the future that imagine a variety of outcomes, usually including both negative and positive possibilities, then checking one's plan against each possible outcome to identify weaknesses.

10. George Lakoff, *Don't Think of an Elephant: Know Your Values and Frame the Debate* (White River Junction, Hartford, VT: Chelsea Green Publishing; 10th anniversary edition, September 23, 2014).

11. Richard H. Thaler and Cass R. Sunstein, *Nudge: Improving Decisions About Health, Wealth, and Happiness* (New Haven, CT: Yale University Press, 2008).

12. Paul C. Nutt, *Why Decisions Fail* (Oakland, CA: Berrett-Koehler, 2002).

13. David Gleicher's formula was first suggested in the 1960s and altered for clarity by Kathleen Dannemiller in the 1980s. I have altered it slightly again to make it easier to remember.

14. Based on the Innovation Journey model presented in *Managing Innovation*, a copyrighted program by Barnes & Conti Associates, Inc., and David L. Francis, Ph.D. (used with permission).

Selected Bibliography

Ariely, Dan. *Predictably Irrational: The Hidden Forces That Shape Our Decisions.* New York, NY: Harper Collins; rev. and expanded ed., 2009.

Chabris, Christopher, and Daniel Simon. *The Invisible Gorilla: How Our Intuitions Deceive Us.* New York, NY: Crown Publishing, 2011.

Heath, Chip, and Dan Heath. *Switch: How to Change Things When Change Is Hard.* New York, NY: Crown Publishing, 2010.

Johnson, Steven. *Where Good Ideas Come From.* New York, NY: Riverhead Books; reprint ed., 2011.

Kahneman, Daniel. *Thinking Fast and Slow.* New York, NY: Farrar, Straus and Giroux, 2013.

Nutt, Paul C. *Why Decisions Fail.* Oakland, CA: Berrett-Koehler, 2002.

Watzlawick, Paul, John Weakland, and Richard Fisch. *Change: Principles of Problem Formation and Problem Resolution.* New York, NY: W. W. Norton; reprint ed., 2011.

Index

Page references in italics indicate a figure.

About the Author

B. Kim Barnes, CEO of Barnes & Conti
Associates, Inc., of Berkeley, California, is
a consultant, author, and entrepreneur. She
has over 40 years' experience in leadership
and organization development, working
globally with organizations in industries
including technology, pharmaceuticals, finance, health care, manufacturing, gov-
ernment, and academia. A frequent speaker
at conferences, Kim has published many
articles in professional journals and books
and is the developer or codeveloper of popular Barnes & Conti programs
such as *Exercising Influence; Constructive Debate; Intelligent Risk-Taking; Managing Innovation;* and *Consulting on the Inside.*

Kim's books include *Exercising Influence: A Guide for Making Things Happen at Work, at Home, and in Your Community, Third Edition* (Wiley, 2015);
Consulting on the Inside: A Practical Guide for Internal Consultants (ATD Press,
2011) with Beverly Scott; and, co-authored with Aviad Goz, *Self-Navigation:
A Compass for Guiding Your Life and Career* (Johari Press, 2013).

In recent years, Kim was inspired to write a tongue-in-cheek corporate mys-
tery series. The first book of the series, *Murder on the 33rd Floor,* was published
in 2012, and the second, *Murder on Retreat,* was published two years later.

Kim graduated from the University of Minnesota and holds a master's degree in human development from the University of Maryland.

Dear reader,

Thank you for picking up this book and welcome to the worldwide BK community! You're joining a special group of people who have come together to create positive change in their lives, organizations, and communities.

What's BK all about?

Our mission is to connect people and ideas to create a world that works for all.

Why? Our communities, organizations, and lives get bogged down by old paradigms of self-interest, exclusion, hierarchy, and privilege. But we believe that can change. That's why we seek the leading experts on these challenges—and share their actionable ideas with you.

A welcome gift

To help you get started, we'd like to offer you a **free copy** of one of our bestselling ebooks:

www.bkconnection.com/welcome

When you claim your **free ebook**, you'll also be subscribed to our blog.

Our freshest insights

Access the best new tools and ideas for leaders at all levels on our blog at ideas.bkconnection.com.

Sincerely,

Your friends at Berrett-Koehler

Certified

Corporation